THE ANGLO-SA
PRINCELY BURIAL
AT PRITTLEWELL,
SOUTHEND-ON-SEA

SUE HIRST AND CHRISTOPHER SCULL

Published in 2019 by MOLA

Copyright © MOLA

A CIP catalogue record for this book is available from the British Library

Editing by Sue Hirst
Copy editing by Simon Burnell
Reprographics by Andy Chopping
Design and typesetting by Sue Cawood
Production by Tracy Wellman

CONTENTS

ACKNOWLEDGEMENTS 4

FOREWORD 5

1 INTRODUCTION 6

2 HOW WAS THE BURIAL STUDIED? 16

3 WHERE WAS THE BURIAL MADE? 22

4 THE BURIAL CHAMBER AND THE MOUND 30

5 WHAT DO WE KNOW ABOUT THE BURIAL ITSELF? 40

6 WHAT WAS BURIED IN THE CHAMBER? 48

7 WHEN WAS THE BURIAL MADE? 80

8 WHAT SORT OF PERSON WAS BURIED? 86

9 WHAT CAN WE SAY ABOUT THE EAST SAXON KINGDOM? 98

FURTHER READING 107

PLACES TO VISIT 108

PICTURE CREDITS 108

Acknowledgements

This book was commissioned by Southend-on-Sea Borough Council from MOLA (Museum of London Archaeology). The text has been compiled and edited by Sue Hirst (MOLA Managing Editor) and Christopher Scull (academic advisor to the Prittlewell project), but is drawn from the full academic report (Blackmore et al 2019: see 'Further reading') and so represents the work and expertise of the many colleagues who collaborated on the excavation and analysis of the Prittlewell burial, and who have contributed to its publication.

MOLA would like to thank Southend Borough Council and Historic England who funded the excavation and post-excavation work. We are also grateful to the British Museum, the Institute of Archaeology of University College London, Southend Central Museum, and to many Anglo-Saxon specialists for help in the study of the Prittlewell finds. The archaeological field team comprised Ian Blair with Dan Eddisford, Gary Evans, Dave Harris, Alexis Haslam, Mike House, Mark Ingram, Andy Leonard, Denise Mulligan, Ashley Pooley, Dave Sankey and Justin Wiles. Conservation was by Liz Barham and Liz Goodman. The principal authors of the academic monograph are Lyn Blackmore, Ian Blair, Sue Hirst and Christopher Scull, with Ken Crowe (landscape history) and Barbara Yorke (historical background). Specialists who contributed to the work are Richard Macphail (soil micromorphology); †Janet Ambers (Raman spectroscopy); Ian M Betts (building material); Amy Thorp (Roman pottery); Lyn Blackmore (prehistoric, Saxon and medieval pottery); Ian Freestone (glass analysis); Noël Adams, Lyn Blackmore, Simon Burnell, Sue Hirst, Graeme Lawson, Marlia Mango, Christopher Scull, George Speake, Leslie Webster and Susan Youngs (artefact research); Gareth Williams (coins); David Starley (ferrous metallurgy); Harriet White with Justine Bayley, Marei Hacke and Duncan Hook (non-ferrous metallurgy); Karen Stewart and Jacqui Watson (wood and other plant material); Damian Goodburn (woodworking); Paul Garside and Angela Middleton (FTIR analysis); Sue Harrington (textile); Esther Cameron with Zoe Knapp (animal-derived remains); Alan Pipe (animal bone); Matthew Collins and Keri Rowsell (ZooMS analysis); Natasha Powers (human bone); and Alex Bayliss, Christopher Bronk Ramsey and Gordon Cook (radiocarbon dating). The project was managed for MOLA by David Bowsher, David Lakin and Nicola Powell. Graphics are by Hannah Faux, Juan José Fuldain, Carlos Lemos and Faith Vardy, with photography by Andy Chopping and Maggie Cox.

FOREWORD

Southend-on-Sea has a fascinating history beginning long before it became a seaside resort in the 1800s. Prittlewell was the medieval village from which Southend grew, but settlement in the area began in prehistoric times and continued through the Roman and Anglo-Saxon periods. The Anglo-Saxon princely burial at Prittlewell is one of the most significant archaeological finds ever made in England. It has deepened our understanding of the time when the Anglo-Saxon kingdoms were being forged and the English were being converted to Christianity; and it places the East Saxon kingdom at the forefront of these crucial developments in politics, culture and belief.

This book accompanies and complements Southend Museums' exhibition of treasures from the burial, offering a distillation of what has been learned from extensive specialist study of the burial – setting out what we know about the person buried at Prittlewell and what they were buried with; and what this tells us about the times they lived in.

Southend-on-Sea Borough Council is proud to have supported the excavation, study and publication of the Prittlewell burial, and delighted that the town will hold and display these finds in stewardship for the nation.

Councillor John Lamb
Leader of Southend-on-Sea Borough Council

1

INTRODUCTION

THE DISCOVERY

In the closing months of 2003 MOLA (Museum of London Archaeology) carried out an archaeological investigation on behalf of Southend-on-Sea Borough Council at Prittlewell, Southend-on-Sea, Essex.

Site location

Roman and Anglo-Saxon burials had been discovered here during the construction of Priory Crescent in 1923, and the aim of the archaeological evaluation was to identify what remains survived and might be affected by a proposed road-widening scheme. On the first day of excavation, an unusually large square pit *c* 4m across, was identified on the east side of the first trench to be opened. Around the edges of the pit, which was filled with yellow-brown sand and gravel, was a darker organic layer that appeared to be the remains of a timber lining. On the second day of excavation this interpretation was confirmed when an ornate copper-alloy hanging bowl was found at the north-west corner of the pit with one of its suspension rings over an iron hook. The bowl was still in its original position, hanging on the wall of a wooden chamber.

Trench 1 being excavated at the south end of the site, with the chamber grave emerging (back right) and an Iron Age ditch (left foreground); view looking north-east

View looking east-north-east across trench 1, showing the pit with the dark inner lining of the burial chamber exposed and the eastern side of the trench extended to include the whole chamber

The hanging bowl on the north wall of the chamber – the first of the grave goods to be discovered (looking north)

The hanging bowl after conservation, showing enamel decoration and decorative strips | Scale c 1:2

View of the burial chamber during excavation (looking east); for the identity of the objects in the chamber see plan in Chapter 6 | 0.50m scale

By the end of the excavation, visitors to the site were amazed to find themselves looking down into a burial chamber with rare metal vessels still hanging from the walls and other items, including a large iron stand, a folding stool, buckets, a large cauldron, elaborate drinking vessels, weapons and a lyre, positioned around the space once occupied by a coffin. Within the coffin, two tiny crosses made of gold foil indicated that this was a Christian, but buried with traditional funerary rites that also embodied pre-Christian and non-Christian beliefs. The evidence of soil layers above the chamber in the east side of the trench showed that it had originally been covered by a substantial mound, long since ploughed flat.

It was clear from the size of the chamber, and the quantity and quality of the grave goods within it, that this was a rare Anglo-Saxon 'princely burial'. Someone of the highest social status had been buried here in the later 6th or early 7th century AD, within an existing cemetery that was also used by people of lesser rank.

This was clearly a find of national and international significance. Only a few such burials are known from Anglo-Saxon England, and Prittlewell is both the best-preserved and the only one to be excavated to the most exacting modern standards. No grave of this wealth and quality had been excavated since the Sutton Hoo ship burial in 1939, and the discovery promised new insights into society and belief at the time when the first Anglo-Saxon kingdoms were being established and the Roman Church was embarking upon the conversion of the English people to Christianity.

View of the site of the burial chamber today with reconstructed mound (looking north-west)

EARLY ANGLO-SAXON ENGLAND

After the withdrawal of Roman imperial government from Britain in the first decade of the 5th century AD, people from lands around the North Sea in what are now the northern Netherlands, northern Germany and southern Scandinavia began to arrive in eastern England, bringing their own language, customs and culture. The monk Bede, writing in Northumbria 300 years later in the AD 720s, recorded the traditions of his time when he said in his *History of the English Church and people* that the newcomers were from three powerful German peoples: the Angles, the Saxons and the Jutes. The first arrivals maintained links with their homelands and were joined by further migrants, and from the second quarter of the 5th century eastern England increasingly became part of this North Sea world. As the leaders of the incomers asserted political control, so the indigenous communities, the descendants of those who had lived in Britain under Roman rule, began to adopt the new ways. From this developed a new cultural milieu that we call Anglo-Saxon, and the adoption of the incomers' language led ultimately to modern English. In western and northern Britain, which did not see migration from the Continent, native leaders were able to establish British kingdoms and to maintain and defend their way of life.

We know most about these early Anglo-Saxons from their distinctive burials. Some were cremated and their remains deposited in the ground, often in pottery vessels; others were laid in the ground unburned, sometimes in wooden coffins. In both rituals they are characteristically found with dress fittings (suggesting clothed burial) and other grave goods. The type and quantity of grave goods symbolised individual status and identity (for example, dress jewellery is almost exclusively found with women, and weapons with men), allowing insights into social structure. In the later 6th and 7th centuries AD, a new level of wealth and ostentation in a small minority of burials, like that at Prittlewell, suggests that society was becoming more stratified and that the social elite had achieved a new level of power and material wealth. It is at this time that historical accounts first mention Anglo-Saxon kingdoms, thought to have been established when a dominant individual was able to unify authority over smaller, less stable political groupings. The kingdom of the East Saxons gave its name to the county of Essex, which was its heartland.

What is a princely burial?

'Princely burial' is a term coined by archaeologists to describe graves so rich and elaborate that they can only be those of the very highest-ranking members of a hierarchical society. They are characterised by grave goods that are exceptional in their number, diversity and high quality, and by substantial burial structures and mounds, all of which emphasise the social and economic distance between ruling elites and their followers.

Such burials have been a recurrent feature of north-west European societies from later prehistory but were a new phenomenon in Anglo-Saxon England in the late 6th and early 7th centuries AD. These Anglo-Saxon burials are interpreted as the resting places of people belonging to the leading families who ruled the new kingdoms.

Burial mounds in the elite cemetery at Sutton Hoo, Suffolk

They can be seen as emphatic statements of power and wealth – warrior lords flaunting their new status and authority. This is often emphasised further by the prominent location of their barrows within the landscape and sometimes by spatial separation from lower-status burials, as in the elite cemetery at Sutton Hoo (Suffolk).

Some of the Anglo-Saxon princely burials were cremations, such as Asthall (Oxfordshire), Coombe (Kent) and Sutton Hoo mound 3. More often the body was buried unburned (inhumed) as at Prittlewell itself, Taplow (Buckinghamshire), Broomfield (Essex), Caenby (Lincolnshire), Sutton Hoo mounds 1 and 2, and Snape (Suffolk) mound 1. Some had been looted in antiquity and others dug up by antiquarian researchers in the 19th century. (In the case of Cuddesdon (Oxfordshire) it is not even known whether the burial was a cremation or an inhumation.) Only Sutton Hoo mound 1 and Prittlewell were both previously undisturbed and excavated to high archaeological standards. Despite our sometimes patchy knowledge, it is nevertheless clear that this small group of elite burials have much in common, and that those who made them used the same types of objects to make statements about the worth and status of the dead. It is no exaggeration to say that they share a common funerary language.

These are the burials of the wealthy and powerful to whom service was owed and from whom rewards flowed. They were the providers, not just partakers, of hospitality, with their suites of drinking and serving vessels, their gaming boards and lyres. The convivial feasting suggested by these finds brings to mind the vivid description

N

Map showing the location of princely burials within the areas of the Anglo-Saxon kingdoms (white type)

0   100km

of a banquet in the great hall called Heorot in *Beowulf*, one of the earliest poems in the English language.

> Then a bench was cleared in that banquet hall
> so the Geats could have room to be together
> and the party sat, proud in their bearing,
> strong and stalwart. An attendant stood by
> with a decorated pitcher, pouring bright
> helpings of mead. And the minstrel sang
> filling Heorot with his head-clearing voice ...
> (*Beowulf*, lines 491–7)

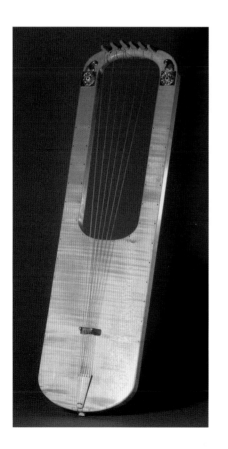

The 1882 excavation of the princely burial at Taplow, Buckinghamshire

Replica of the Sutton Hoo lyre

2

How was the burial studied?

Excavation is only a part of archaeological investigation. When fieldwork ends, a whole range of further tasks and analyses, collectively termed post-excavation work, are needed to ensure that the full story is understood and made as widely available as possible through publication and museum displays.

The archaeologist in charge of the site will analyse the excavation records to work out the precise sequence of events that formed the archaeological layers. Attention will be paid to documents and maps in local archives, as well as local archaeological publications, which may assist in the interpretation of the history of the site in its local landscape. Other experts will also be consulted. For Prittlewell, soil scientists studied samples from the mound and the chamber fills, using the techniques of soil micromorphology, to see what this could tell us about the ground where the burial was made, how the mound was built, and how the chamber filled up. Experts in ancient timber working considered how the chamber might have been constructed, and engineers helped to calculate the size of the mound and the strength of the roof timbers needed to support it. Osteologists studied the small fragments of human tooth enamel and animal bone recovered during the excavation.

Meanwhile the finds will have been assessed with several considerations in mind. Do they need conservation? What sorts of specialists will be needed to study them? What drawings and photographs should be made? What kinds of scientific analyses should be undertaken to obtain the maximum information from the objects found? MOLA conservators worked closely with the archaeological team throughout the excavation and were responsible for lifting most of the fragile objects in their surrounding soil, and with their fills intact, for detailed excavation and recording in the laboratory. Soil blocks and their contents were X-rayed before further laboratory investigation so that the conservators had a better idea of what to expect as they

Maple-wood bottles with
ornamented neck fittings in their
soil block in the laboratory, with
(behind) X-radiograph of the same

removed the soil from the artefacts. Because they were so dense, standard X-rays did not work well on the soil blocks containing the sword and the lyre, and so these were also given computer tomography (CT) scans. The two faces of the lyre were also recorded by laser scanning before the wood fragments and metal fittings were removed from the soil for conservation treatment. Conservation at MOLA is carried out under guiding principles of minimum intervention and reversible treatment. Where possible, conservation measures are preventive rather than interventive, and non-destructive analyses carried out.

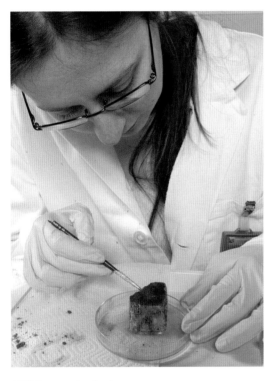

A MOLA conservator cleaning
one of a pair of antler dice in
the laboratory

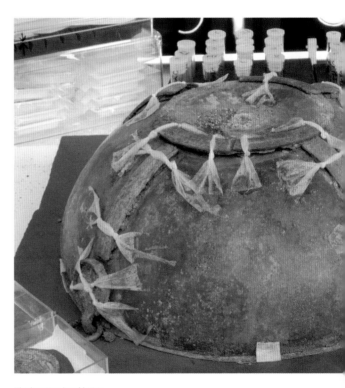

The hanging bowl being
reassembled in the laboratory
during conservation

Laser scanning of the lyre in its
original soil block at MOLA, with
the resultant image showing on
the screen behind

Conservation and specialist study of the objects necessarily go hand-in-hand. The quality and diversity of the artefacts found meant that MOLA conservators worked alongside experts in the analysis of ancient glass, iron, copper alloy, silver and gold working technologies and of organic materials, as well as specialists studying particular artefacts or artefact types, such as the lyre, weapons and vessels. The east Mediterranean flagon became part of a study of similar flagons carried out at the British Museum.

Organic materials that would normally decay completely can be preserved by contact with corrosion from iron, copper-alloy and silver objects. In the case of iron, corrosion products replace organic material to form a fossil-like cast, while with silver and copper alloy the corrosion products can also prevent bacterial decay. Almost every metal object in the burial bore such organic traces, offering tantalising evidence of a range of items that had otherwise completely disappeared. These were studied by experts in textiles, wood and woodworking, plants and the use of animal-derived materials such as bone, horn and hide.

The specialist analyses often required advanced scientific techniques. For example, X-ray fluorescence (XRF) and scanning electron microscopy with energy dispersive X-ray spectroscopy (SEM-EDS) were used to study the composition of copper, silver and gold alloys. Raman spectroscopy was used to identify pigments, and showed that garnets in the lyre fittings are almandines, probably from India or Sri Lanka. Zooarchaeology by mass spectrometry (ZooMS) was used to determine the species of animal bone too poorly preserved to be identified by eye, by the chemical signature of its collagen. Radiocarbon dating and statistical modelling proved critical in determining the date of the burial.

All of this information was essential to build up a full picture of the burial and answer the big questions that it poses. Who was this person? When did they live and die? And what sort of world did they live in? Organising the different strands of work, and integrating the results, was a complex business. A team of 43, including archaeologists, conservators, scientists and historians from universities and other museums as well as from MOLA, plus photographers and graphic artists, collaborated on piecing together the story of the Prittlewell burial and bringing it to publication.

Opposite, left: A portable X-ray fluorescence (pXRF) machine being used in the laboratory to determine the composition of the gilded copper-alloy fittings
Opposite, right: A group of flagons (the Prittlewell example left front) being analysed by X-ray fluorescence (XRF) at the British Museum

Opposite, left: An expert in animal-derived material examining a sample with a binocular microscope in the laboratory
Opposite, right: An expert in mineral-preserved wood examining the iron coffin fittings to see what can be learnt about the coffin structure from the wood remains on the fittings

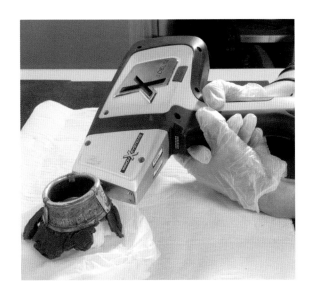

3

WHERE WAS THE BURIAL MADE?

THE SITE – TOPOGRAPHY AND HISTORY

Prittlewell lies at the south-centre of the Southend peninsula in south-east Essex, on the south-east side of a shallow valley where the Prittle brook bends to flow north into the River Roach. This pleasant valley, with water, fertile land and shelter from the exposed Thames estuary to the south, has been settled since the prehistoric period. Earthworks of a Late Bronze Age or Early Iron Age defended settlement lie on the north side of a ridge of higher ground running north-east from the site. To the south is the medieval church, which incorporates remnants of a Saxon predecessor. To the west of the site, the precinct of an early 12th-century Cluniac priory (Prittlewell Priory, now parkland) straddles the Prittle brook.

A Saxon blocked doorway in
the north wall of the chancel
of St Mary's church, Prittlewell

Detail from Chapman and
Andre's map of 1777, showing
the Prittlewell area and
South End

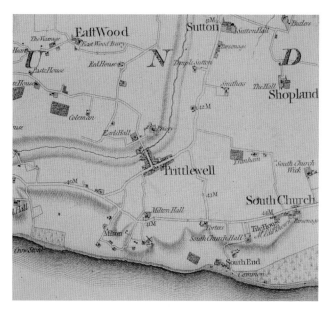

About 2km (1.25 miles) to the south, on the Thames estuary, the hamlet of South End (of Prittlewell) grew up around a break in the cliffs, where the low gravel hills of south Essex reach the river. In 1801 South End had 51 houses and was already something of a sea-bathing resort. In 1856 the London, Tilbury and Southend Railway was opened and the growth of Southend-on-Sea as a London commuter town began. The Great Eastern Railway line, which opened in 1889, allowed a northwards expansion of Southend. Construction of the railway disturbed Anglo-Saxon burials at Prittlewell, evidenced by the find of an Anglo-Saxon spearhead in 1887. In 1923 Anglo-Saxon and a few Roman burials were found during road building (the construction of Priory Crescent).

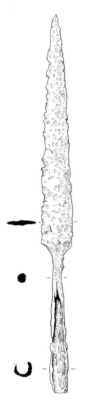

The iron spearhead found in a railway cutting at Prittlewell in 1887 | Scale 1:4

Workmen excavating archaeological features on the site during the construction of Priory Crescent in 1923

Artefacts found with a Roman cremation burial in 1923
Height of glass bottle 290mm

More Anglo-Saxon grave goods were found during further work on the railway cuttings at Prittlewell in 1930–1, including items from three female burials: a pair of saucer brooches and a string of beads dated to the second half of the 6th century AD, a gold pendant of the 6th century with stamped and repoussé decoration, and a gold pendant dated to the mid 7th century with filigree and cloisonné garnet decoration. It was William Pollitt, then Borough Curator and Librarian at Southend Museum, who monitored, recorded and then published these and the earlier finds. Finally, in 2003 one certain and one possible weapon burial were found to the north of the princely burial chamber.

A pair of gilded, copper-alloy saucer brooches with amber, glass and crystal beads, found in 1930 | Scale 1:1

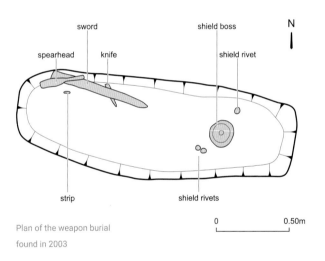

Plan of the weapon burial found in 2003

The burials lie at the west end of the west–east ridge mentioned above. These lower slopes dipping down to the south, to marshy ground to the north and to the Prittle brook to the west, were locally prominent features before modern development and landscaping, as shown in a photograph taken during construction of what is now Priory Crescent, looking north towards the Eastern Avenue railway bridge (below).

Circular gold pendants, one with filigree and cloisonné garnet decoration (Pollitt 1930A) and one with stamped and repoussé decoration (Pollitt 1930B), found in 1930 | Scale 1:1

Blue glass globular beaker
Scale c 1:2

Small hand-made pottery
bottle | Scale c 1:1

Two small wheel-thrown pottery
beakers, found in 1930 | Scale c 1:4

Iron shield boss, found
in 1931 | Scale c 1:2

mound

View looking north along
the line of Priory Crescent
during pipe laying and major
landscaping works in advance
of road construction in 1923,
showing the position of the
mound of the princely burial

The cemetery ridge lies north of the Thames watershed, in the catchment of the
Roach, and there is no view southwards to the Thames estuary from the cemetery.
Site location and topography may, therefore, suggest that this was the burial ground
of a community whose immediate sense of place was focused on the Prittle brook
and the Roach valley to the north, rather than the land to the south overlooking the
Thames estuary. There was, however, easy access to the Thames where the cliffs
break at Porters creek and the fishing village of South End developed; boats could
easily be beached here at any period. With the Prittle brook flowing into the tidal
estuary of the River Roach to the north-east, a community at Prittlewell would have
had good access to coastal communication routes along the Thames and to Kent
and the Continent on the one hand, and along the east coast to north-east Essex,
Suffolk and Norfolk on the other.

THE CEMETERY

The minimum extent of the burial area, c 170m by 65m, can be inferred from the
known distribution of graves and grave goods, and from topographic considerations.
Burial may have extended beyond the easternmost finds made during works on the
railway cutting in 1930–1 and further west towards the Prittle brook in what is now
Priory Park. It is unlikely that the burial area extended much if at all beyond the
northern limits of the 2003 evaluation because of marshy low-lying ground. To the
south, no finds are known to have been made during the construction of Priory
Crescent south of the railway bridge or the houses on its eastern side, suggesting

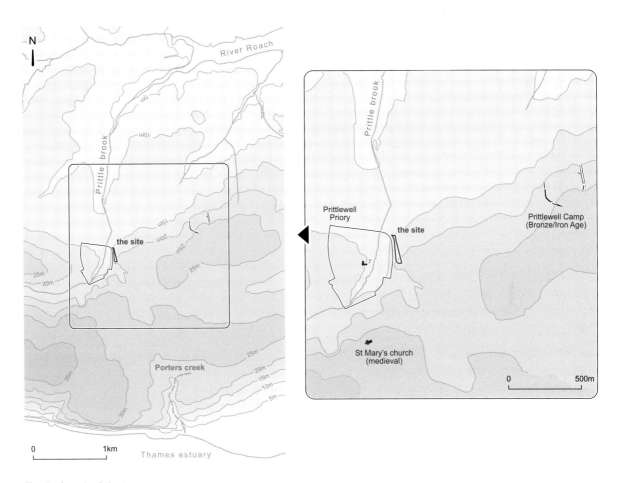

The site shown in relation to local topography and the Late Bronze Age or Early Iron Age Prittlewell Camp, medieval church and priory

that the artefacts found close to the railway bridge in 1930 were at the southern limit of burials.

The combined finds and observations from 1887, 1923, 1930–1 and 2003 represent at least 34 inhumations, in addition to the chamber grave; other observations and material may bring this total to as many as 41–43 burials. The recorded inhumations probably represent between one fifth and one quarter of those originally buried here, including burials probably destroyed without record during railway construction. This indicates that 150–200 individuals were buried here during the century or so that the cemetery was in use.

Burial began here in the second half of the 6th century AD and continued into the middle or third quarter of the 7th century. The chamber grave, which is dated to the late 6th century (Chapter 7), is not the earliest burial and appears to have been deliberately placed within or adjacent to an existing cemetery of flat graves (that is, inhumations without mounds over them) that continued to be used. It had a locally prominent situation on a low promontory, overlooking the flat cemetery, and its mound would have been visible from the north and west. Whether it was a single monument or part of a group is not known, but it is possible that there were further burials under mounds here, and the filigree gold-and-garnet pendant (find-spot 1930 south of the A1159) might possibly have come from one of these.

The number of burials and the length of time that the cemetery was in use suggest that it served a community of 30–60 individuals. Both men and women were buried here, but while the recorded material represents at least 23 and possibly as many as 28 male weapon burials, it is possible to identify securely no more than five or six female burials. This may indicate that there were more men than women in the community using the cemetery or that there was a preference for burying men here. It is equally possible, though, that this apparent gender imbalance, and the absence of children, is more apparent than real. The finds from 1887–1931 were recovered during construction work, not during controlled archaeological excavation, and it is very likely that some less obvious finds and smaller bones were not seen or not recognised.

The cemetery at Prittlewell represents a high-status community with access to costly weapons and jewellery (and the skills to produce them), precious metals and imported goods. It was established during the third quarter of the 6th century AD, a time of social and political change associated with the early development of the Anglo-Saxon kingdoms. Some of the artefacts found suggest social or political contacts with the powerful kingdom of Kent, and access to the maritime and coastal exchange systems that linked south-east England and the Continent. It is impossible to be certain whether this was a community of multiple families or households with a normal population structure, or one with a majority of adult males such as might be expected of the household of an elite leader with a high proportion of warrior retainers, but the evidence perhaps favours the second alternative.

Plan of the cemetery showing
oriented graves and all finds
with the suggested minimum
extent of the cemetery

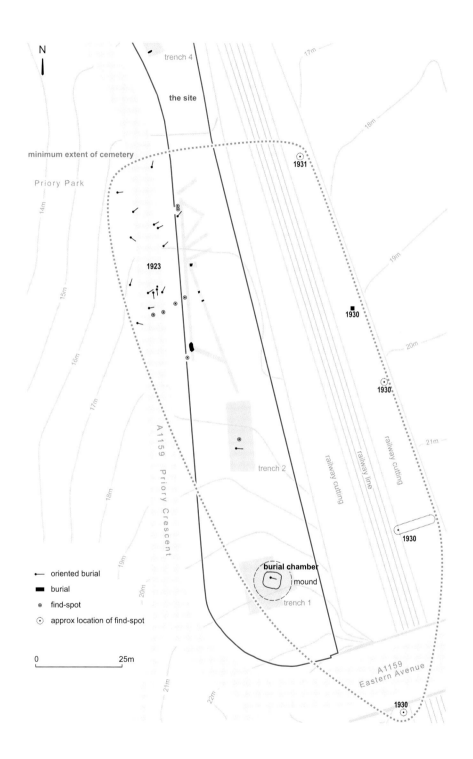

N

trench 4

the site

minimum extent of cemetery

1931

Priory Park

1923

1930

1930

trench 2

railway cutting

railway line

railway cutting

1930

A1159 Priory Crescent

•—— oriented burial

■ burial

⊙ find-spot

◉ approx location of find-spot

0   25m

burial chamber

mound

trench 1

A1159
Eastern Avenue

1930

4

THE BURIAL CHAMBER AND THE MOUND

THE BURIAL CHAMBER

When excavating the burial chamber, the archaeologists had to be aware that the complex fill of what had been a wood-lined subterranean space would preserve evidence for the construction of the chamber and mound, and for their subsequent decay and collapse. Determining the original structure of the chamber was difficult because the timbers had completely decayed, leaving only greyish-brown soil stains. However, by combining the evidence of excavation with analysis of soil samples and organic material preserved on some of the metal artefacts in the chamber, it has been possible to reconstruct in some detail how the chamber was put together and the woodworking technology that it represents.

CONSTRUCTION PIT

Once the place for the burial chamber had been chosen, the footprint of the proposed mound was stripped of turf and topsoil, and then levelled to form a construction platform.

The construction pit for the burial chamber measured *c* 4.35m (east–west) by 4.00m (north–south) and was *c* 1.4–1.5m deep from the prepared Anglo-Saxon ground surface. It is likely that the excavation of this pit, in soft natural sand, would have only taken a day or two for unskilled labourers to complete. By far the greatest investment in terms of time, skill and labour was the cutting and shaping of the large boards and timbers needed to construct the chamber.

WALLS AND BASEPLATE STRUCTURE

Evidence for the chamber walls had been recognised at the beginning of the excavation but it was the mineral-preserved wood (Chapter 2) surviving on the iron hooks hammered into the wall, and on some of the metal items hung from the hooks, that provided crucial information. The orientation of the woodgrain showed that the walls of the chamber were made of radially-cut oak planks around 50mm thick that were set upright on end. Planks of this thickness would almost certainly have been 1/16th sections cleft from large logs. They were probably joined edgewise with tongue-and-groove joints (radially-cut boards, with a slightly wedge-shaped section, are particularly suitable for this).

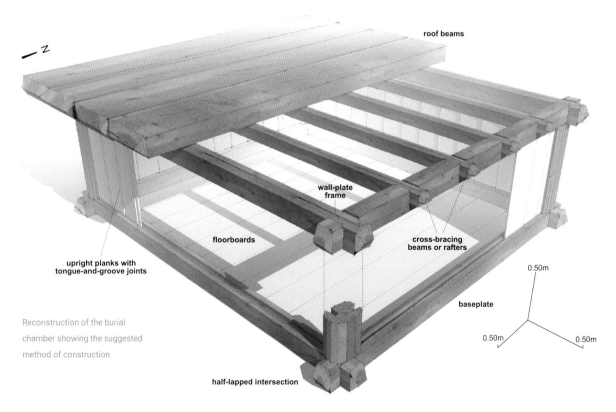

An iron wall hook showing vertical woodgrain on the pointed end that had been driven into the chamber wall

Scale 1:2

There is no direct evidence for their width but it is likely that the boards were 300–400mm wide and that 36–48 of them were needed to build the walls. There are two pieces of evidence for the original height of the walls. The tallest object in the

roof beams

wall-plate frame

floorboards

cross-bracing beams or rafters

upright planks with tongue-and-groove joints

baseplate

0.50m

0.50m

0.50m

half-lapped intersection

Reconstruction of the burial chamber showing the suggested method of construction

chamber was the iron stand in the north-east corner that, at 1.33m tall as reconstructed, provides a minimum height for the underside of the roof. The surface of the prepared ground on the north (downslope) side of the chamber, which was probably the level of the top of the wall and so also the underside of the roof timbers, was c 1.4m above the base of the chamber.

There is no evidence for a beamslot cut into the base of the chamber and so it is likely that the bases of the vertical boards were originally held in slotted baseplate timbers. Evidence for such a baseplate was preserved as a horizontal band of mineral-preserved oak against the bottom iron hoop of one of two wooden buckets positioned in the south-east corner of the chamber. The corner intersections of the baseplates are likely to have been half-lapped over one another; there was room in the corners of the chamber pit for the projecting ends of the beams. It is assumed that a similar bracing frame would have retained the tops of the boards at ground level in the same fashion as a wall plate on a building. The structure was probably further supported by corner posts with side grooves for the plank walling.

The incomplete upper part of the iron stand surviving *in situ* in the north-east corner of the chamber, showing its relationship to the top edge of the excavated chamber

0.20m scale

FLOOR

The base of the pit was covered by a thin homogeneous organic deposit interpreted as the remains of a wooden floor. Evidence for the floor structure comes from small fragments of oak in soil samples or preserved in the corrosion layers of metal objects resting on the bottom of the chamber. For example, preserved woodgrain on the lower iron handle of the large cauldron ran north–south, indicating that this was the orientation of the floor timbers.

Another indication that the floor was boarded was the consistent horizontal level of the grave goods that were found in place across the base of the chamber, something that would have been hard to achieve had the soft natural sand been left exposed during construction of the chamber and the subsequent furnishing of the burial. As there is no evidence for joists, it is most likely that the floorboards were laid directly on the surface of the sand and simply butted against each other and the baseplates.

Plant remains on the base of the chamber suggest floor coverings. There are fragments that might be from woven rush and grass matting, and indications that parts of the floor may have been strewn with cut grass and loose plant material (Chapter 6).

ROOF

Three parallel soil stains, aligned north–south across the eastern half of the chamber, represent the remains of three adjoining roof timbers (the largest c 0.6m wide). There was no evidence that the chamber had a pitched roof, or for internal supporting posts. There is, however, some evidence for supporting beams. Two parallel east–west timber stains, each 0.20m wide, were found under the remains of the roof timbers and above the east end of the coffin. They are interpreted as the remains of collapsed east–west beams notched over the wall plate to help to brace

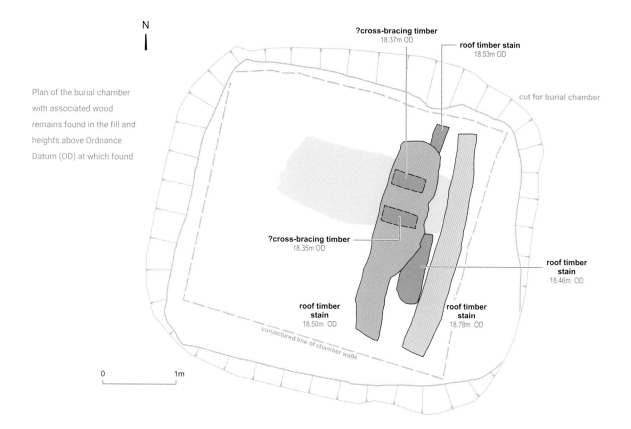

N

?cross-bracing timber
18.37m OD

roof timber stain
18.53m OD

cut for burial chamber

Plan of the burial chamber with associated wood remains found in the fill and heights above Ordnance Datum (OD) at which found

?cross-bracing timber
18.35m OD

roof timber stain
18.46m OD

roof timber stain
18.50m OD

roof timber stain
18.78m OD

conjectured line of chamber walls

0   1m

and retain the east and west walls of the chamber and support the roof. The roof timbers, which were of a length to span the chamber and strong enough to support the mound, were laid side-by-side on a north–south alignment, supported by the wall plate, beams and the ground surface beyond. They were probably jointed in some way to prevent soil from the mound falling between them and an axe-cut rebate would have been the simplest way to do this.

The beams would have obstructed views of and access to the burial chamber. They and the roof would have been installed once the burial ceremony was complete and the chamber was being sealed.

THE RESOURCES NEEDED TO CONSTRUCT THE CHAMBER

The construction of the chamber represents a considerable investment of labour, skills and materials.

The baseplates, wall plates and corner posts were probably made from two medium-sized tall oaks, easier to find than the very large straight-grained 'board' trees needed for the wall uprights. A work team of four could have felled and prepared the baseplate and wall plate beams in perhaps two days, with a further day for the corner posts.

Three logs at least 1.6m long and *c* 1m in diameter would have been needed to produce 48 wall planks 300mm wide from ¹/₁₆th radially-cleft sections. They would have weighed *c* 1.3 tonnes each and the cleaving and rough trimming of the boards, if not the whole process of making them, would almost certainly have been done where they were felled. The manufacture of the wall planks, from finding, felling and bucking the three parent logs, through radial cleaving and trimming, could have been done by three small work gangs (one for each log) of perhaps up to four adults each, producing the 48 boards in *c* 25–30 person days.

Turning a log into ¹/₁₆th radially-cleft boards

The floorboards, which were not load-bearing, may have been relatively light radially-cleft boards perhaps c 30mm thick. These could be produced from about half a large 'board' log of c 1m diameter, which could yield 32 boards with an average trimmed width of c 0.3m. Such a log would have weighed c 2.8 tonnes. If there were 12 boards, each a 1/32nd split section, a gang of four skilled workers could probably have roughly finished them from the standing tree in two days, a total of eight person days. However, this work rate would only have been possible with near-perfect board logs of c 1m diameter.

Engineering calculations indicate that the roof timbers must have been at least c 200–250mm thick if they were to bear the weight of the mound. These were the most substantial timbers used in the chamber and were probably hewn from cleft half logs from large straight oaks providing logs c 0.75m in diameter at the mid length. The individual roof timbers would have weighed nearly 0.5 tonnes. A team of four skilled workers could have made the eight timbers from standing trees in two and a half days (representing ten person days of labour), followed by some time to move the heavy timbers to the burial chamber site (perhaps one day with local labourers helping).

The cross-bracing beams were each hewn from a parent log c 0.35m in diameter at the mid length. The individual beams would have weighed c 0.4 tonnes. Following trimming, the weight of the individual beams would have been reduced to c 0.17 tonnes. Four skilled workers could have made the beams from the standing trees in two days (eight person days of labour).

For the final fitting and assembly of the woodwork, perhaps a couple of days would be needed. The minimum size of the work gang can be estimated from the weight of the roof timbers, each weighing nearly half a tonne. Using skids, levers and rope these could have been dragged into position by as few as four people but, if carrying was required, then as many as eight to ten strong adults would be needed. As speed would have been desirable, it is likely that the optimum rather than the minimum labour was deployed.

The construction of the chamber was thus a complex business, with several work gangs, perhaps as many as six, engaged in producing different timbers for the structure. These gangs would probably have been dispersed over quite a large area and done most of the work where the trees were felled (as many as 10–14 trees might have been needed, depending on their size). They would then have come together, with any necessary additional labour, for the fitting and jointing of the timbers *in situ*, when the burial pit had already been excavated by unskilled labour. A force of 20–25 woodworkers, including some experienced treewrights and some unskilled labour, could have dug the pit, made the timbers and erected the chamber in as little as five days. The oak would have been worked when green, which is much easier and quicker than working partially dried or seasoned wood.

THE MOUND

After the burial chamber was closed, a mound was raised over it. Nothing of the mound survived at the modern ground level, but there was evidence for it in the side of the trench, where a build-up of soil above the Anglo-Saxon ground surface had preserved the profile of the mound after it collapsed into the burial chamber. This suggests that the mound was originally 11–12m across and 2.0–2.5m high. A mound of this size would have needed considerably more soil than that dug from the chamber construction pit and, as there was no evidence for a surrounding ditch or for quarry pits, it seems likely that the turf and topsoil removed during ground preparation from the area of the chamber grave would have been used. Building the mound might have taken ten labourers around two days.

The Prittlewell mound, at 11–12m across, was small compared to those of other princely burials in England. The Asthall mound was at least 17m in diameter, Caenby *c* 33m, Taplow *c* 24m and Sutton Hoo mound 1 *c* 30m. Original heights are difficult to estimate, but Prittlewell would have been proportionately lower and less impressive than these. The Taplow mound as excavated was *c* 5m high but had clearly been altered over time. The original height of Sutton Hoo mound 1 has been estimated at *c* 4m, and the Caenby mound was reportedly 8ft (*c* 2.4m) high when excavated.

Original section across the eastern edge of the chamber grave and its collapsed mound being cleaned for recording (looking south-east), with explanatory section drawing below

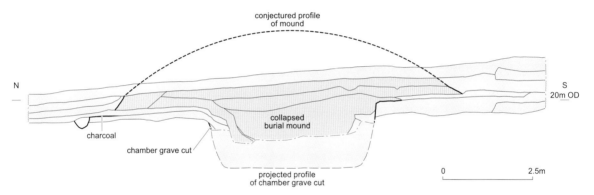

conjectured profile of mound

N

S
20m OD

charcoal

chamber grave cut

collapsed burial mound

projected profile of chamber grave cut

0   2.5m

DECAY AND COLLAPSE

There is no evidence that the chamber was ever re-entered or otherwise disturbed, and it remained intact for a long time, probably for centuries, after the grave was sealed. Over time the overlying mound material gradually filtered into the burial space as the roof timbers slowly decayed, partially filling the chamber and holding vessels hanging on the wall in their original positions. When the roof timbers finally gave way the mound collapsed into what was left of the void, and was then further reduced by erosion and ploughing over the centuries to a point where it was no longer visible.

The free-draining sandy soil surrounding the burial chamber would have facilitated the passage of moisture and oxygen (depending on drier or wetter conditions) through the structure – key factors in the decay of the chamber. The rate of decay would have accelerated once the protective envelope of the massive chamber structure was broken, when the roof finally collapsed.

The first breach in the roof was in the north-east corner where local decay of the roof timbers allowed soil from the overlying mound to filter into the void; over time this built up into a sloping fan-shaped deposit within the chamber. When the roof finally failed, the northern and eastern part settled onto this fill but the southern and western part collapsed more violently into the deeper underlying void. The effects of this are clearly seen in the greater displacement and damage to objects in the western part of the chamber, most notably the head end of the coffin that was not protected by the build-up of material from the mound and was, therefore, vulnerable. Smaller items affected by the collapse include the wooden box that was found upside down, its painted lid against the floor of the chamber, having evidently been knocked over from its original position (below, Chapter 6).

Excavation of the chamber in progress, showing the sloping fan-shaped deposit with (back right) the undulating surface of collapsed north–south roof timbers over it (looking south-east)

5

What do we know about the burial itself?

The coffin

A **wooden coffin** with **iron fittings** was placed west–east in the northern half of the chamber. Although the wood had decayed, leaving just a soil stain, the mound material that had partially filled the chamber had built up around the sides of the coffin, preserving its shape as a void and holding some of the fittings in place. The coffin was best preserved at its east end, where wood survived against the large copper-alloy cauldron. The soil stains of three boards, aligned along the length of the coffin, showed where the lid had collapsed into the base.

Low-level view of the coffin and the surrounding filtration deposits with collapsed angle brackets (looking east)

Plan of the coffin evidence
within the chamber, showing
the position of the iron coffin
fittings as found and the soil
marks of timbers

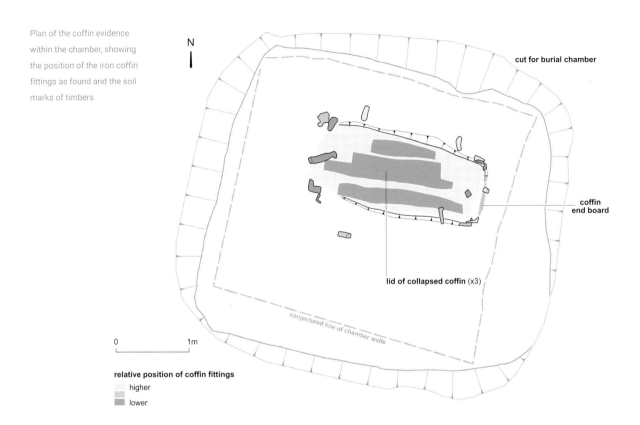

N

cut for burial chamber

coffin
end board

lid of collapsed coffin (x3)

conjectured line of chamber walls

0   1m

relative position of coffin fittings
higher
lower

The east end of the coffin,
showing corner angle
brackets *in situ* and wood of
the end board preserved
against the base of the large
cauldron | 0.20m scale

The coffin was 2.25m long and 0.85m wide, and c 0.5m high. It would have been joined together with wooden pegs, and the corners and lid were reinforced with 16 L-shaped iron angle brackets. Wood preserved on the brackets and the nails that fastened them shows that the coffin was made from ash boards that were at least 40mm thick. The sides, head and foot may have been made from paired or single boards (our reconstruction shows single boards) and the lid was made of three longitudinal boards reinforced at either end with a cross board. There is no evidence for the construction of the base.

Woodgrain preserved on the angle brackets shows that the boards of the coffin came from at least three large ash logs (the coffin sides, if single boards, would have come from a log 2.3–2.4m long and c 0.6m wide). Finding and felling the trees, preparation of the boards and construction of the coffin represent perhaps 8–13 person days' work for woodworkers working as a pair or in a larger group. The iron fittings represent further skilled labour.

This was an exceptionally large coffin and would have weighed around 160kg. Iron coffin fittings are rare at this time, but coffins with angle brackets are known from

Iron lamp found in the coffin area and probably originally placed on the lid | Scale c 1:4

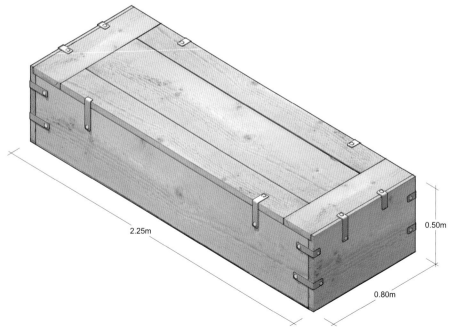

2.25m

0.50m

0.80m

Reconstruction of the ash-wood coffin with angle brackets and lid in position burials in Kent and the Merovingian Frankish kingdoms in present-day France and the neighbouring countries. Both the size of the coffin and the use of iron fittings might be explained by the importance of the person buried here. The size and weight of the coffin would have made it difficult to manoeuvre, and it was probably lowered into the chamber first and other objects then placed around it.

The remains of an **iron lamp** were found at the east end of the coffin. It is formed of a bowl, which originally probably contained oil or beeswax and a wick, on a stem with four splayed feet. Lamps of the same sort were also found in the princely burials at Broomfield and Sutton Hoo mound 1.

There were remains of **textiles** on the iron clamps that secured the coffin lid. It appears that the coffin lid was covered with cloths, probably cloaks (Chapter 6), and the lighted lamp then placed on the coffin at its east (foot) end.

THE BODY AND ITS ACCOUTREMENTS

Human bone did not survive in the environmental conditions of the burial chamber and no traces of the skeleton were found other than fragments of **tooth enamel**. These were recognised after excavation in soil samples taken from the west end of the coffin space, and confirmed that the body had been buried with the head to the west and feet to the east, the normal orientation at this time. It was possible to identify crown fragments from permanent molars from a single individual. Permanent molars mean that the individual must have been more than 6 years old at death but no more accurate age can be established. The size of the coffin suggests that the individual was probably fully grown, or nearly so, and stature estimated from the position of dress fittings within the coffin supports this (below).

Two small **gold-foil crosses**, each 27mm long, were found side-by-side at the head end of the coffin. Their position suggests that they were placed over the eyes of the deceased and there is no evidence, such as thread holes, that they were attached to a cloth or garment. Clearly of Christian significance, the crosses are a unique find in England and difficult to parallel anywhere. Gold-foil crosses are known from burials of the late 6th to early 8th centuries AD in southern Germany and northern Italy, but these are usually equal-armed, highly decorated singletons, and were sewn to cloth or garments. By contrast the matching pair of Prittlewell crosses are smaller, undecorated, of Latin cross form and were not attached to a cloth backing.

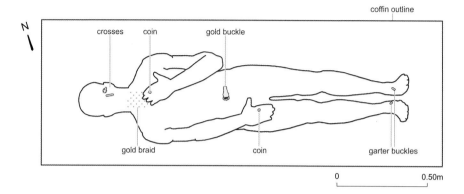

Plan of the coffin area showing the position of the artefacts in relation to the conjectured body

The gold-foil crosses
Scale 2:1

The gold-foil crosses during excavation, with a gold coin in the centre and the gold belt buckle at far left (looking south)

Immediately east of the crosses, in the chest region of the burial, was a small section of gold thread. This was block-lifted and when X-rayed revealed a delicate woven **gold braid**. This was probably the edge of a piece of luxury cloth laid over the face and neck, masking the features and helping to keep the crosses in place.

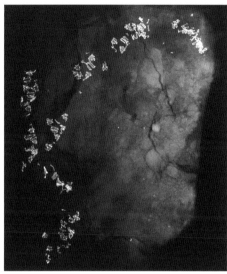

Reconstruction drawing of the gold braid | Scale 1:1

Loose fragments of gold-foil threads from the gold braid
Scale 2:1

X-radiograph of gold braid *in situ* in the chest region of the burial | Scale 1:2

Near the gold braid was one of two **gold coins**, with the second found lower down the coffin in the area of the right thigh. Both are Frankish gold *tremisses*, a coin worth one third of the gold *solidus*. They are of the 'mint-and-moneyer' series, so-called because they carry the name of the moneyer who issued the coin on one side and the name of the town or city in which the coin was minted on the other. However, they do not identify the ruler in whose reign they were issued and so cannot be closely dated unless they bear the names of moneyers for whom there is other independent dating, or the specific type occurs in a hoard with more precisely datable coins. Neither is the case here. The coin found in the chest area was issued by the moneyer Ioannes (John) of Cadolidi and that by the thigh by the moneyer Vitalis of Paris. Coins of the 'mint-and-moneyer' series were produced c AD 580–675 and both Prittlewell coins were struck within the earlier part of this period.

Gold coin found
in the chest area
Scale 2:1

Gold coin found in the
area of the right thigh
Scale 2:1

The largest and most striking object found within the coffin was the **gold belt buckle** in the area of the waist. Triangular belt buckles of this type are known from the later 6th and early 7th centuries AD but not usually in gold. This example shows no signs of wear and in some critical places is too fragile for everyday use. It seems likely that, like the gold crosses, it was made especially for the burial. A gold belt buckle may have had a particular symbolic significance for high-status male identity. Larger and more elaborate gold belt buckles were found in the princely burials at Taplow and Sutton Hoo mound 1.

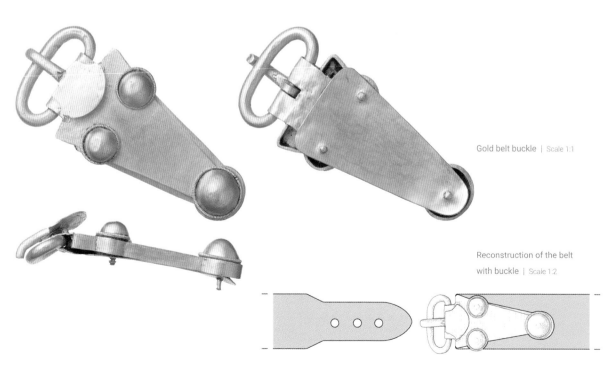

Gold belt buckle | Scale 1:1

Reconstruction of the belt
with buckle | Scale 1:2

Two tiny **copper-alloy garter buckles** with rectangular plates and counter-plates were found at the east (foot) end of the coffin, further confirming the orientation of the body. These would have been attached to leather cross-garters, probably tied below the knees over stockings or gaiters, crossed over the calves and ankles, and then around the insteps, with the buckles fastened over some sort of light leather shoes. They are very plain examples of the type.

The body was thus clothed, with gold-foil crosses over the eyes and a fine cloth covering the face and neck. The presence of the gold belt buckle and the absence of female dress accessories such as brooches, beads or pendants indicate a male. Assuming that he was laid out on his back, the distance between the crosses and the garter buckles indicates that the deceased was around 1.73m (5ft 8¼in) tall, and so an adult or older juvenile. If the coins were placed in the hands then the right arm was extended along the side of the body and the left arm flexed across the chest.

Other personal possessions that would normally be worn on the body at the belt, such as the knife and firesteel, were buried separately outside the coffin together with further items in a maple-wood box (Chapter 6). The placement of the weapons, away from the body and coffin, is also unusual.

Copper-alloy garter buckles with counter-plates (extant buckles, with plates as on X-radiograph), with reconstruction showing a buckle fastening gartering over a light shoe
Object drawings scale 1:1

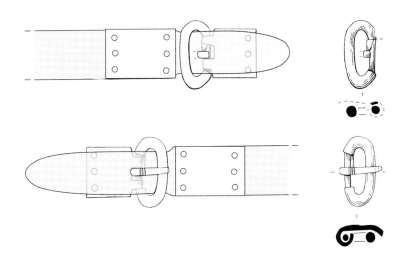

6

WHAT WAS BURIED IN THE CHAMBER?

INTRODUCTION

The coffin itself was by far the largest object in the burial chamber and once in place would have obstructed easy access to the north wall and the north-east corner. The hooks above the coffin were, therefore, most probably fixed to the walls before the coffin was lowered into the chamber. Once it was in position the other objects were arranged around the chamber to form the burial tableau – that is, the formal display of coffin and grave goods in the burial chamber that was intended to convey to mourners and onlookers the status, identity and social connections of the deceased and his kin.

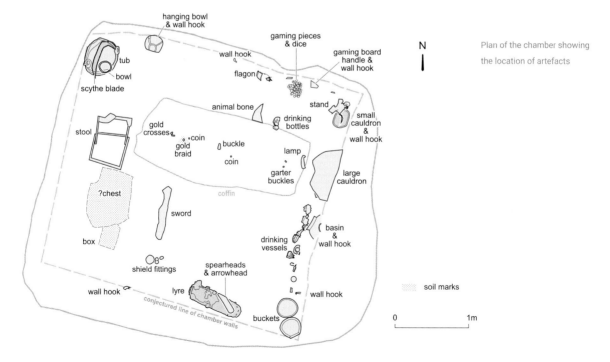

Plan of the chamber showing the location of artefacts

The smaller and more fragile items, notably the drinking vessels along the east wall, were probably arranged once the large objects, such as the great cauldron, were in place. There was an empty area south of the coffin and this was probably the access point for those furnishing the chamber, with the tableau intended to be viewed from the south. It is tempting to suppose that the last object added as part of the funeral rite was the lamp, placed on the coffin immediately before the final roof timbers were put in place sealing the chamber.

OBJECTS HUNG ON THE WALLS

Ten **iron hooks** and a **wooden peg** were used to hang a variety of objects on the chamber walls. Seven hooks were found still in place, three holding vessels still in their original positions. All were set 0.5–0.8m above the chamber floor, perhaps to heighten the visual impact of the suspended items when viewed from above.

Three hooks were found in place on the north wall. The westernmost supported the ornate **copper-alloy hanging bowl** with enamelled mounts, which was made by craftsmen in western or northern Britain and was probably acquired as a gift. Textile remains on the central hook may suggest that a garment was hung here. East of this, and in position on the wall, was a **copper-alloy flagon**. No hook was found with this and it may have stood on a small shelf. The flagon was made in the eastern

The eastern Mediterranean flagon *in situ* during excavation

0.10m scale

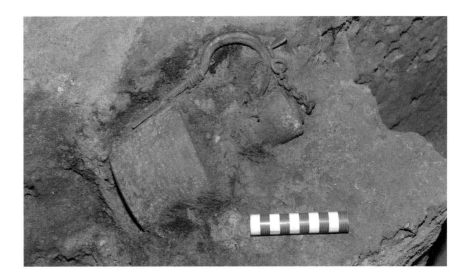

Mediterranean, most probably in Syria. Around its neck is a band with three medallions with a relief image of St Sergius on horseback; such items were acquired by pilgrims to the shrine of Sts Sergius and Bacchus at Resafa in Syria. It belongs to a broad group of hammered copper flasks, jugs, flagons and other containers common within the Byzantine Empire, and found mainly in Asia Minor and the Levant, but rare in western Europe. It is unlikely that it arrived directly from the eastern Mediterranean, and more likely that it passed through several hands before arriving in what is now Essex, again very probably as a gift.

An iron handle fitting was corroded to the easternmost hook on the north wall and two decorated iron mounts were found nearby. These appear to be fittings from a **wooden gaming board**

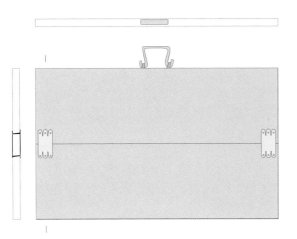

Reconstruction drawing of the gaming board showing the position of the handle and mounts | Scale 1:10

Copper-alloy flagon from the eastern Mediterranean, with detail of a saint on horseback from one of the discs on the neck band | Scale of flagon c 1:2

that was hung up by its handle, and this interpretation is supported by 57 **whalebone gaming pieces** and two large **antler dice** found immediately below on the chamber floor. These were in a tight group and were probably contained in a bag hung from the same hook. They are the best-preserved organic items from the burial, and their good condition is probably due to localised waterlogging from water penetrating through the decayed roof timbers at the north-east corner. Gaming equipment has been found buried with higher-status Anglo-Saxon men, for example in the Taplow princely burial, but the Prittlewell find is unusual in being a complete or near-complete set. We do not know exactly what games it was used for, but the combined presence of counters and dice suggests both games of skill (war games) and games of chance (racing games).

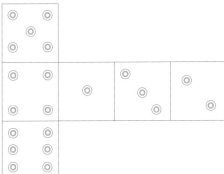

Antler dice with diagram showing the arrangement of the numbers | Scale 1:2

Whalebone gaming pieces
Average diameter c 31mm

At the north end of the east wall was hung a **small copper-alloy cauldron**, probably used in the preparation and serving of food or drink. To the south of this a very **large copper-alloy cauldron** (625mm in diameter) lay on its side between the foot of the coffin and the wall. This was originally hung on the wall from an oak peg, but when the peg gave way the cauldron slipped down to the floor. Both vessels were made by a process of hollowing and raising from a single piece of sheet metal. Similar large cauldrons were found in the princely burials at Sutton Hoo mound 1 and Taplow. These great cauldrons with their rounded bases were cooking vessels intended to be suspended over a fire from a chain attached to the ring handles. Their size, and their association with only the highest-status male burials, both suggest the capacity to provide for large numbers of people at great feasts. The food cooked in them may perhaps have included broths, gruel made of vegetables and grains, and stews containing meat.

South of the large cauldron was a cast **copper-alloy basin** hung on an iron hook by one of its two drop handles. Made in the eastern Mediterranean as a water basin

The small copper-alloy lugged cauldron hung on a hook being excavated in the north-east corner of the chamber

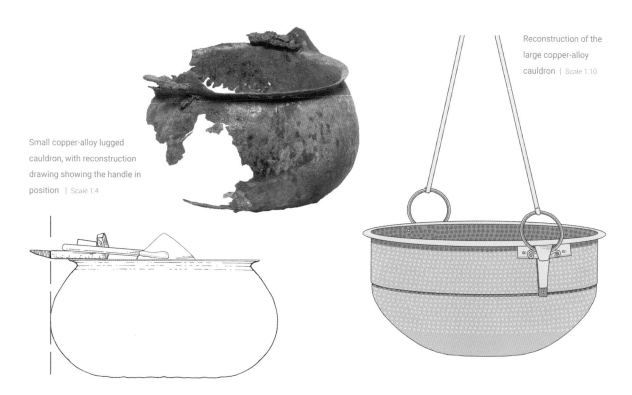

Small copper-alloy lugged cauldron, with reconstruction drawing showing the handle in position | Scale 1:4

Reconstruction of the large copper-alloy cauldron | Scale 1:10

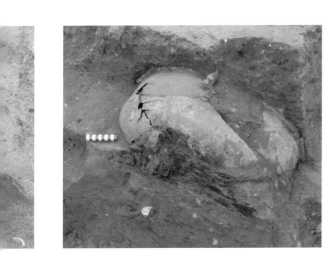

The large copper-alloy cauldron
in situ against the east wall of
the chamber | 0.10m scale

Excavation of the copper-alloy basin
on the east wall of the chamber;
note the drop handle still held in
place over an iron wall hook

used for washing, it stands on a plain raised foot. Such vessels are a feature of elite burials in England, with examples also known from Asthall, Taplow and Sutton Hoo mound 1. Like the flagon, this is evidence that the kin of the person buried here had access to items from the eastern Mediterranean through networks of trade or gift exchange, or both.

Remains of a relatively lightweight **textile** on the iron hook at the south end of the east wall suggest that an article of clothing was hung here.

The eastern Mediterranean
basin | Scale c 1:4

Only one hook remained in place on the south wall, towards the west end, but a second was found close to the east end of the south wall, corroded to the sockets of two **iron spearheads** that, with an **iron arrowhead**, overlay the lyre (below) on the floor of the chamber. It would appear that the spears and arrow were bundled together and racked on the south wall, with the wooden spear shafts supported by the western hook, and that at some point the heads of the weapons had fallen, together with the hook supporting them. The spears are remarkable for the carved decoration on the mineral-preserved remains of the wooden shafts. The similarity of the two-strand interlace within the split of the sockets suggests that these were intended to be a matching pair; the shaft of one spear also had a horizontal band of animal ornament featuring the head of a creature whose U-shaped head and jaws are turned back to bite its own body.

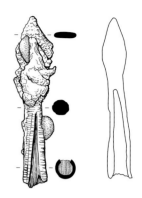

Iron arrowhead | Scale 1:2

The remains of a **shield**, represented by iron fittings, were found face down on the floor below the western hook on the south wall. The surviving fittings are a shield boss, a reinforcement for the hand grip, two disc-headed mounts (there were probably originally four, perhaps suggesting that the shield had taken some damage

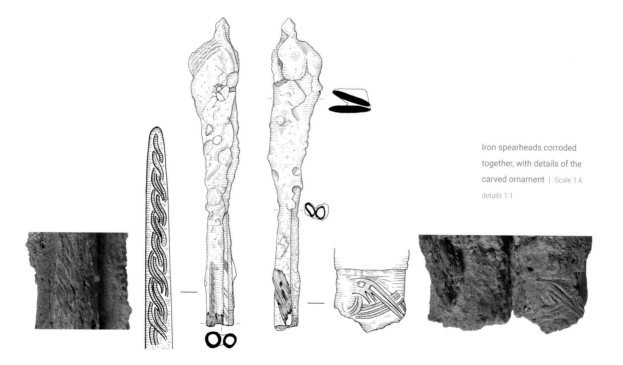

Iron spearheads corroded together, with details of the carved ornament | Scale 1:4, details 1:1

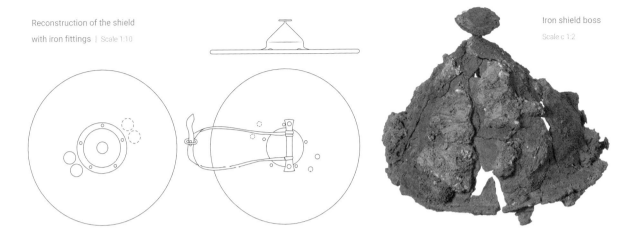

Reconstruction of the shield with iron fittings | Scale 1:10

Iron shield boss
Scale c 1:2

before it was buried) and the buckle from an adjustable strap. The only decorative element is the silver sheet on the disc at the apex of the shield boss. Organic remains preserved on the iron fittings show that the shield board was of willow or poplar wood, covered with hide or leather. The shield appears to have been hung on the wall hook and fell when the leather strap rotted.

There were originally two hooks on the west wall but both had fallen out. One was found corroded to one of the feet of the folding stool (below). The second was inside the large tub, beneath an **iron scythe blade**. It seems probable that the scythe, like the spears, was racked on two hooks and that its blade fell with one hook into the tub when the shaft decayed. The scythe blade is a very rare find for this period. An implement used specifically for mowing grass or hay, its presence suggests the ownership of livestock, particularly stabled horses.

The scythe blade as found inside the iron-bound tub

scythe blade

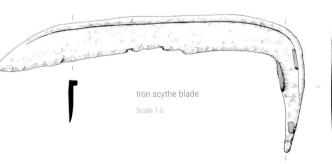

Iron scythe blade
Scale 1:6

The drinking vessels

An array of drinking vessels was placed along the east wall of the chamber south of the large cauldron: two wooden bottles, a pair of drinking horns and three wooden cups, all with elaborately decorated metal mounts, and a pair of blue and a pair of green glass beakers. Another pair of wooden bottles with decorated metal mounts was placed separately on the north side of the coffin. None of the organic vessels was complete, but enough wood or horn had been preserved by contact with the metal fittings to indicate the size and form, and to allow identification to species.

Glass beakers, wooden drinking vessels with decorative metal rim mounts and a drinking horn as found along the east wall of the chamber | 0.10m scale

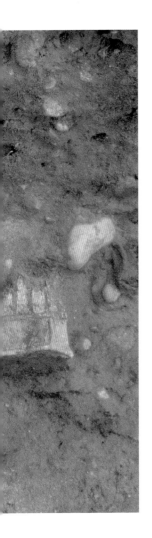

Most of the drinking vessels on the east side of the chamber were found in or very close to their original positions, but there is evidence that some had moved. The glass beakers were lying on their sides, suggesting that they may have tumbled from a slightly higher level, and one of the wooden bottles was upright over one of the drinking horns, which can only mean that they were originally placed at different levels in the chamber. One possibility is that some of the vessels were placed on a shelf attached to the upper surface of the baseplate that held the vertical wall timbers, and the others just below this on the floor.

A pair of wooden bottles with elaborate decorative metal rim mounts placed to the north of the coffin

The two **blue glass beakers**, with trailed lattice decoration on the body and trailed lobed decoration on the base, are a rare type and are so similar that they were almost certainly made as a matching pair. Almost all known beakers of this colour and form come from high-status burials, suggesting that they were specially made for the social elite. The two **pale green glass beakers** are of a much more common type, with spiralling trailed decoration around the neck and vertical loops creating a rosette at the base. They are smaller, and much less alike, than the blue pair. All four glass vessels were probably made in Kent.

Blue and green glass beakers

Scale c 1:2

Seven-lobed trail on the base
of a blue glass beaker

Scale 1:2

Immediately south of the glass beakers was a pair of **maple-wood bottles** with gilded metal fittings. Gilded copper-alloy panels decorated with die-impressed animal interlace were secured to a rim binding by fluted silver-gilt clips, with a fluted silver-gilt strip along the base of the panels.

Maple-wood bottles with decorative rim mounts from the main drinking vessel array

Scale *c* 1.1

Next to the bottles was a pair of **drinking horns** with gilded copper-alloy fittings. Below a C-sectioned rim binding is a broad horizontal band made of three rectangular panels of die-impressed animal interlace, secured to the horn lip by three rim clips in the form of a stylised horse's head; these cover the joins between the panels. Below the band are 12 pendent triangles, also decorated with die-impressed animal interlace, pinned to the horn, with the junction between the band and triangles covered by a fluted strip. Horns of this size, as indicated by the rim diameters, can only be from cattle – perhaps domestic, but perhaps from the aurochs (*Bos primigenius*), a large wild species once native to Europe but now extinct. Aurochs horns would have been larger and more sharply curved than those of domestic stock, and may have had a rarity value.

Detail of a horse-head rim clip
Scale 2.1

One of the pair of drinking horns | Scale c 1.2

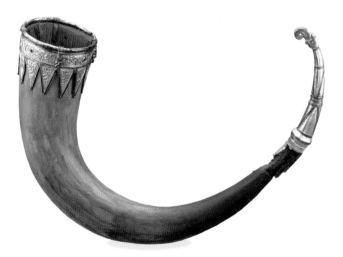

Drinking horn fittings from the princely burial at Taplow, Buckinghamshire, mounted on a modern horn and showing how the Prittlewell rim fittings might have looked

At the south end of the line of drinking vessels were the remains of three **wooden cups**. A matching pair made of burr maple (then, as now, burr wood was prized by woodworkers for its decorative grain) had simple gilded copper-alloy rim bindings secured to the rim by fluted rim clips whose terminals are ornamented with bird heads. The fragmentary remains of a third cup had silver rim bindings.

Matching pair of wooden drinking cups with pendent bird-head terminals on the rim clips | Scale c 1:1

The pair of **maple-wood bottles** placed on the north side of the coffin had gilded silver fittings. The panels forming the decorative band around the neck are the same as those on the two bottles found on the east side of the chamber, but like the drinking horns they also have pendent triangles. The latter are decorated with animal interlace and a stylised human face.

The richly ornamented drinking horns, decorated bottles and cups, and glass beakers were luxury items, intended to impress when used in public displays of hospitality. The use of the same die in the decoration of all four bottles indicates that they were made or adorned by the same craftsmen, possibly as part of a larger set. The range of different vessel types may reflect their use for different drinks (perhaps ale, mead and wine?) and the pairing of vessels – implying more than one drinker – symbolises the expectation of company and the obligation to provide hospitality. It was not uncommon for one or two drinking vessels to be included in the burials of higher-ranking people, but the number and range at Prittlewell is exceptional, comparable only with the princely burials at Taplow and Sutton Hoo mound 1.

The two bottles by the coffin were deliberately placed away from the rest of the drinking set. There was a joint of beef beside them (below) and it may be that this food and drink for the dead was the deceased's portion of a funeral meal.

Detail of the design on the pendent triangle mounts of the wooden bottles | Scale 2:1

Pair of wooden bottles found beside the coffin | Scale c 1:1

Standing items and objects placed on the floor

In the north-east corner was an **iron stand**, still intact and upright on its four feet but with some damage from the collapse of the roof timbers. It terminates in a central prong and two triple-pronged side arms. The main shaft is twisted in alternate directions and the side arms in one direction. This is a unique find in Anglo-Saxon England but belongs to a rare group of items known more widely in Europe and the Mediterranean world, which are related to Roman and Byzantine lighting equipment, and it would probably have functioned as a candelabrum. In contrast to the lamp on the coffin, such stands would have been used to light larger spaces and have had a decorative function as display pieces. It is easy to envisage how several might have been arranged to light the interior of a hall, for example.

The iron stand *in situ* in the north-east corner of the chamber | 0.20m scale

The iron stand with detail showing the reconstructed branching arms at the top

Scale c 1:10, detail c 1:2

Two **wooden buckets** with iron hoops, collars and handles stood in the south-east corner of the chamber next to the group of drinking vessels. One was made of yew staves and the other, more unusually, of larch wood. They may have contained drink to be served in the drinking vessels. Traces of cereal bran in the base of one bucket may suggest ale.

 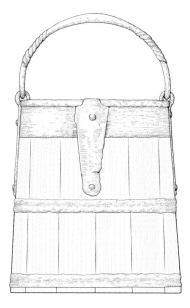

Reconstruction drawings of the pair of buckets from the south-east corner of the chamber | Scale 1:6

One of a pair of iron-bound wooden buckets found in the south-east corner of the chamber, after conservation
Maximum (compressed) height c 240mm

In the north-west corner stood a large **yew-wood tub** with iron hoops, collar and ring handles. Similar tubs are known from other burials of high-status men, including Sutton Hoo mound 1. We have already seen that the scythe blade fell from the wall into the tub, but also found in the tub was a **copper-alloy bowl**. This was probably made in the Meuse valley or the Rhineland in modern France or Germany and was originally acquired as a piece of fine tableware. However, it had been repaired and may have had a secondary use as a dipper to ladle out the contents of the tub, perhaps water.

Copper-alloy bowl inside the
tub | External rim diameter 161 x
175mm

Iron-bound tub after
conservation, with profiles
showing slumping of the iron
bands as the wooden staves
decayed | Maximum
(compressed) height 366mm

Reconstruction drawing of
the tub | Scale 1:6

On the south side of the chamber, lying on the floor parallel to the south wall, were the remains of a **lyre**. The lyre (Old English *hearpe*) was the most important type of stringed musical instrument in the ancient world. It has a hollow sound box attached to a frame of two arms connected across the top by a bar, or 'yoke', to which the upper ends of the strings are attached and tensioned by means of rotating pegs. The strings run over a bridge, a small arched device that stands on the centre line of the sound board and conveys their vibrations to the sound box for amplification.

The wooden structure of the instrument had almost completely decayed, leaving a soil stain with the metal fittings preserved in their original positions and some fragments of wood. The remains were lifted in a soil block for excavation and examination in the conservation laboratory. This is the first time the complete form of an Anglo-Saxon lyre has been recorded.

The lyre lay face down. It was made of maple, with ash tuning pegs, and traces of animal hair preserved on the metal fittings indicate that it was buried within an animal-skin bag, as was the lyre from Sutton Hoo mound 1. There were two sets of metal fittings: those that were part of the original construction of the instrument and those that had been used in repairs after serious damage.

The dark soil mark on the floor of the chamber representing the lyre (looking east), with the iron spear bundle over it (left)
0.10m scale

Plan of the lyre as found and moved to the laboratory in a soil block, with the back face uppermost | Scale 1:6

▨	gilt fitting
▨	silver fitting (back)
▨	copper-alloy fitting
▨	iron fitting
▨	visible wood fragments
▨	lyre soil stain

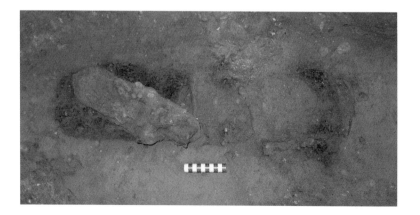

The original metal fittings were two circular mounts of gilded copper alloy decorated with interlace and with central garnet inlays, two fluted silver bands, and an iron loop, attached to the foot of the instrument by a leather strap, that acted as a tailpiece to secure the strings; traces of the strings were preserved on the corroded iron. No trace was found of the bridge. Between the arms were copper-alloy fittings with the remains of a leather strap. This would have been looped around the wrist to support the instrument, freeing both hands to pluck and stop the strings.

Copper-alloy fittings and leather from a suspension strap for the lyre | Scale 1:1

Reconstruction drawing of the lyre, with detail of a silver fluted fitting and one of the gilded copper-alloy decorative mounts

Drawing at 1:8, details 1:1

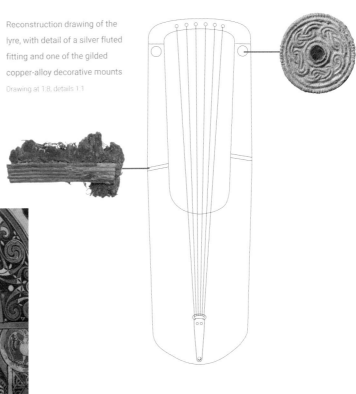

King David the psalmist playing the lyre surrounded by his musicians; detail of a full-page miniature from the early 8th-century AD Vespasian Psalter

Two iron bands had been riveted to the yoke, apparently to correct a serious structural failure, and metal fittings had been used to repair a crack that ran right through the sound board and the sound box on the front and back. The repair fittings were fluted silver strips on the front and gilded copper-alloy strips on the back. Both sets were attached by means of rivets fixed through small backplates on the inside surface of the sound box and sound board. This would have involved the sound box being dismantled and put back together again. Evidence of tiny iron pins holding the sound board to the sound box was also found. It is not clear how the lyre was damaged but the repairs had been carried out very skilfully.

The only evidence for when the lyre was made is the decoration on the circular mounts, which suggests manufacture in the 50 years or so before it was buried. It may have been a personal instrument, implying musical skill on the part of the deceased, but is more likely to be symbolic of a lord's cultural patronage and public persona. In the non-literate society of the time, tradition and traditional knowledge were preserved and transmitted orally in song and poetry. The lyre was an instrument of public performance in the feasting hall, and when this included panegyric (poetry in praise of the lord, his kin, or his forebears) the bard (Old English *scop*) was an agent of propaganda and oral diplomacy.

Reconstruction drawing of the lyre showing the front (right) and back faces with repair fittings, and detail of silver and gilded copper-alloy repair plates *in situ* over a crack in the wood | Drawing at 1:8, details 1:1

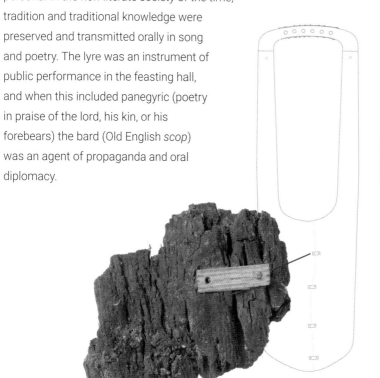

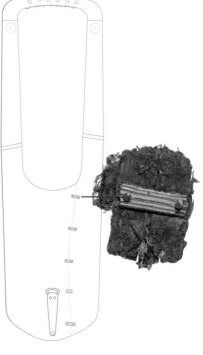

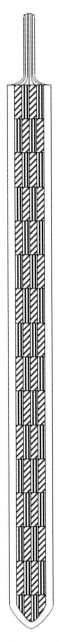

A **sword** was placed on the floor south of the coffin with its hilt towards it. Organic traces preserved on the iron of the blade and tang showed that the hilt fittings were of horn, and that the sword had been housed in a scabbard made of thin ash staves with a fleece lining and a covering of hide or leather. The fleece lining held the blade tightly and the lanolin in the raw wool greased the blade and kept it bright. The blade was pattern-welded, a technique whereby the smith constructs the blade from multiple strips of piled and twisted iron rather than from a single billet of metal. This was intended to give the blade resilience, and leaves highly decorative complex twisting patterns on the polished surface. In this case 64 individual iron rods were twisted and piled into four strips that were then forged together to make the core of the blade, to which the cutting edges were then welded. The only metal fittings on the hilt are two collars of ribbed gold wire at either end of the grip. More, and more elaborate, sword fittings might have been expected but the swords from the princely burials at Taplow and Broomfield both had plain horn hilts with no metal fittings at all. The Prittlewell sword is a large pattern-welded blade that represents a considerable investment of skill and materials, and the gold hilt fittings, although modest when compared to those from Sutton Hoo mound 1 or the Staffordshire hoard, signal an aristocratic or royal status.

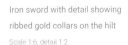

Iron sword with detail showing
ribbed gold collars on the hilt
Scale 1:6, detail 1:2

Schematic diagram of the
construction of the sword
blade

On the west side of the chamber, near the head of the coffin, was an **iron folding stool**. Material from the mound had accumulated to a depth of *c* 0.2m beneath the stool before the seat rotted and the frame slumped downwards.

The frame is formed of two U-shaped pieces joined at the axis by dome-headed pivot pins and strengthened by upper and lower stretchers. Although there are several different sorts of textile preserved on the stool, none is from its seat, which was probably of leather. This was attached by being looped over two retractable iron rods that could be slotted through loops on the top of the frame. The reconstruction indicates the original height of the stool and two possible alternative arrangements for the leather seat.

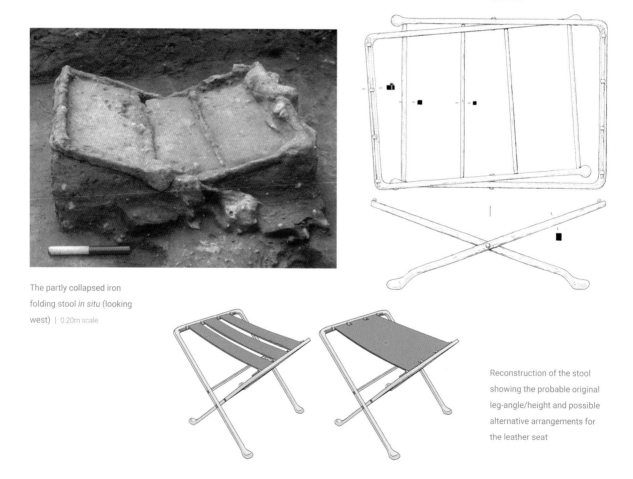

The iron folding stool as found
Scale 1:10

The partly collapsed iron folding stool *in situ* (looking west) | 0.20m scale

Reconstruction of the stool showing the probable original leg-angle/height and possible alternative arrangements for the leather seat

This type of portable camp stool was associated with the military and with magistrates in the Roman period. Later pictorial and literary evidence from Anglo-Saxon England suggests that the Prittlewell stool might be a *gif-stol* (gift seat) from which the lord dispensed rewards and judgement to his followers, and thus a symbol of rulership or lordly authority.

Immediately south of the stool, soil staining and differences in the fill suggested an organic object that had otherwise wholly decomposed. The shallow deposits that had accumulated north and east of this object preserved the shape of a corner and vertical sides, from which it appears that this was a **wooden chest**. The less regular shape south of this suggests crushing and displacement by falling roof timbers.

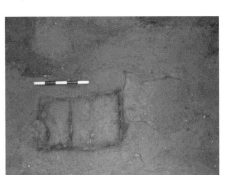

The outline of the soil mark next to the folding stool (to left) when first exposed (looking east) | 0.50m scale

The rectangular ?chest when almost fully excavated, with the stool to the left and the black rectangular shape of the smaller box complex adjoining its right-hand edge (looking east) | 0.20m scale

Immediately south of the chest was a cluster of metal objects surrounded by a roughly rectangular dark organic stain. This was lifted in a soil block for excavation in the conservation laboratory and proved to be the remains of a **maple-wood box** containing objects that appear to be intimate personal possessions.

Some wood from the box survived, preserved by the proximity of silver and copper alloy, and was found to be painted, a unique survival from this time. The restricted range of colours – red and yellow ochre, and white from gypsum – is similar to that used in some manuscripts. The two elongated oval shapes, one with cross-hatching possibly suggesting scales, may be swimming fish. The yellow ladder pattern resembles the border decoration of some Anglo-Saxon gold-and-garnet jewellery, and may have been intended to evoke this.

The painted surface of the box was underneath the metal objects, facing down. The base of the box may have been painted, but it seems more likely that this was the lid. If so, its inverted position means that it must have fallen or been displaced from a higher position nearby. Most probably, the box was originally placed on the wooden chest, and was knocked over when the roof timbers collapsed. The contents remained close together, suggesting that the box was still intact when it was displaced.

Painted wooden box fragments | Scale 1:1

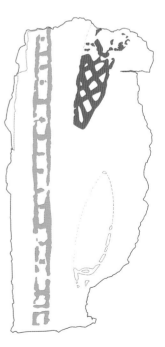

Inside the box was a **silver spoon** of Roman or Byzantine form that, like the flagon and cast basin, had been made in the eastern Mediterranean. Scratched on the bowl of the spoon are a cross (probably an ownership mark) and what appear to be three names – 'FABI' ([property of] *Fabius*), 'BRIT' (perhaps *Brittus/a* or *Britto*) and 'ROMN' or 'ROMAI' (perhaps indicating *Rom(a)n(us)*) – indicating that the spoon had had several owners. Next to the spoon was a small **copper-alloy cylindrical container**. These are not common but are known from burials in England and on the Continent, most often of women and juveniles, frequently of high status. The Prittlewell container is a relatively early and small example, and is unusual in being from a male grave. These were probably amulet containers, and some have been interpreted as relic containers when found in a Christian context.

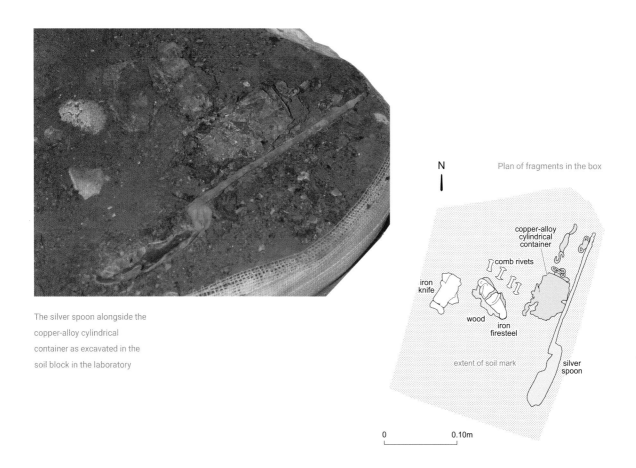

The silver spoon alongside the copper-alloy cylindrical container as excavated in the soil block in the laboratory

Plan of fragments in the box

N

copper-alloy cylindrical container

comb rivets

iron knife

wood

iron firesteel

extent of soil mark

silver spoon

0   0.10m

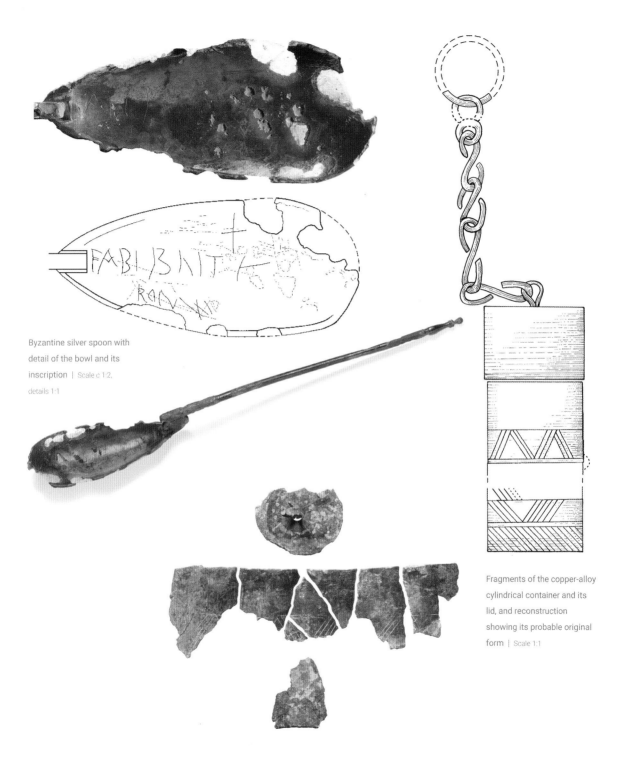

Byzantine silver spoon with
detail of the bowl and its
inscription | Scale c 1:2,
details 1:1

Fragments of the copper-alloy
cylindrical container and its
lid, and reconstruction
showing its probable original
form | Scale 1:1

Other items in the box were an **antler comb** (identified from a row of small iron rivets on which antler traces were preserved), an **iron knife** with the remains of a horn handle and sheath, and an **iron firesteel**. Textile remains on the comb rivets and cylindrical container indicate that there was also **cloth** in the box. This may have been simply to wrap the contents but might have been an article of clothing, perhaps an undergarment. The remains of a **beech-wood disc**, found under the firesteel, may be the lid of a small cylindrical box. The firesteel may have been in this, perhaps with tinder material such as dried moss.

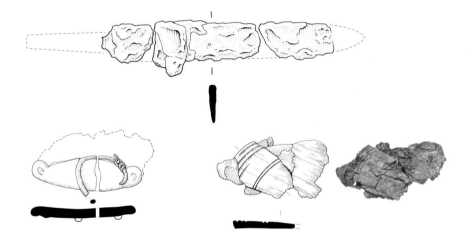

Iron knife and firesteel with part of the wooden disc lid from an associated container

Scale 1:2

ANIMAL REMAINS AND FOOD OFFERINGS

A very poorly preserved piece of cattle bone (the species identification confirmed by ZooMS), found with the two wooden bottles by the north side of the coffin, was all that remained of a **joint of beef**. Fragments of animal teeth found elsewhere in the chamber are almost certainly from earlier domestic refuse in the soil that was used to build the mound and so have nothing to do with the burial itself.

Textiles and soft furnishings

Although the surviving evidence is relatively poor when compared with Sutton Hoo mound 1 and Taplow, it is clear that **cloth and textiles** formed a major component of the burial assemblage at Prittlewell.

Outside the coffin, textile remains on 35 metal objects represent at least 19 different types of cloth. None of these, however, were wall hangings. There are textile remains on three wall hooks but all are probably from garments, with that hanging from the same hook as the east Mediterranean basin perhaps being a cloak.

The coffin was covered by at least four cloths, possibly cloaks. A number of different finely-woven cloths, and perhaps a cushion, appear to have been placed on the seat of the stool and perhaps on the nearby wooden chest. Further textiles lay over the sword. These included two rare types, a basket weave that was possibly an heirloom cloth, and a twill cloth that may have been imported. Textile remains on the cone of

Detail of a fine-weave textile, possibly from an inner garment, on an iron wall hook on the south wall of the chamber | Scale c 2:1

The 2/2 diamond twill on a coffin bracket showing diamonds running horizontally
Extent of textile 30 x 23mm

Plain weave, closely woven with a ribbed effect, on the outer edge of the top rail of the stool frame at the west end of the stool | Extent of textile 65 x 15mm

the shield boss indicate that the shield was either covered by, or fell onto, several layers of cloth. The stand, hanging bowl and small lugged cauldron, and the mouths of the tub and buckets, may also have been cloth-covered. Covering the mouths of vessels might be seen as a practical measure to protect their contents and may even have been a common feature of their everyday use. It is tempting to suppose that other items, apart from the coffin, were left uncovered until shortly before the closing of the chamber, when covering them with cloth might be seen both as protecting them and to symbolise closure at the conclusion of the funeral rite. Whatever the sequence, the quality, texture, colours and disposition of the cloths would have significantly enhanced the visual impact of the burial tableau.

Mineral-preserved remains of **plant fibres** that appear to have been woven or plaited were found on the shield boss and the lyre where they lay on the chamber floor, suggesting that there were grass or rush mats here. There were also plant fibres below one of the drinking horns and the large cauldron, and on the foot of the stool. In two cases these can be identified to the grass family, with one fragment of possible club-rush, suggesting grass or meadow cuttings on the chamber floor.

Weave diagram with chevron design observed in plant stems found under the lyre
Photograph 2:1, drawing 1:1

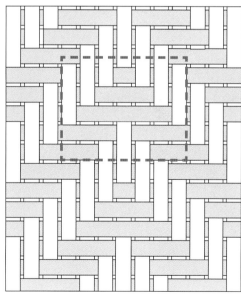

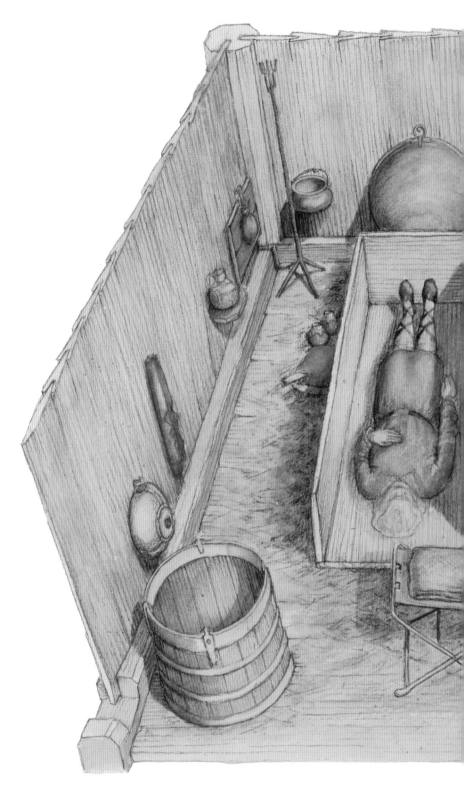

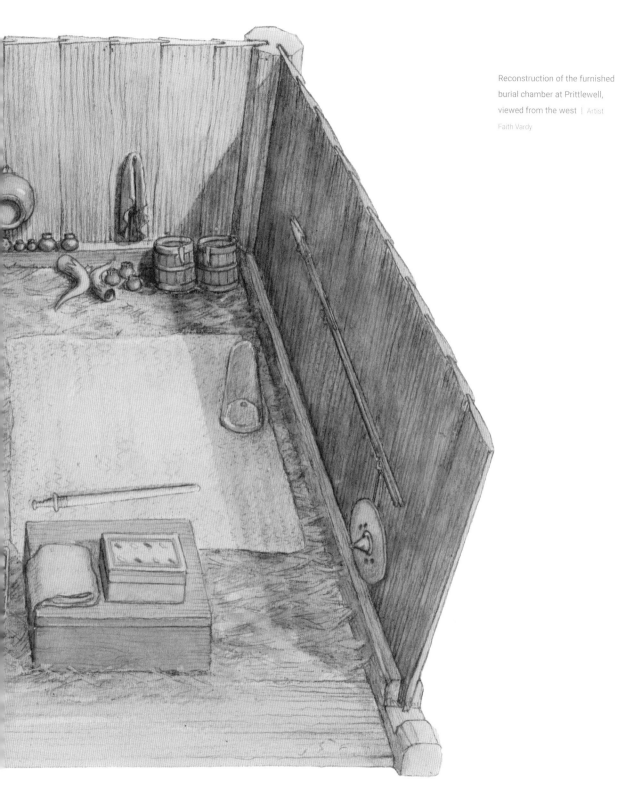

Reconstruction of the furnished
burial chamber at Prittlewell,
viewed from the west | Artist
Faith Vardy

7

WHEN WAS THE BURIAL MADE?

THE COINS AND ARTEFACTS

The artefacts in the chamber were collected together and buried in the later 6th or the earlier 7th century AD. None of the objects need have been made any later than this, and there are no items that would be characteristic of a date any later in the 7th century. Three factors are particularly important when we try to estimate the date of the burial from the objects it contained.

The gold coins, although they cannot be precisely dated to a year or a reign, are most likely to have been circulating in the period c AD 580–630.

The animal ornament on the drinking vessels and spear shafts is in 'Salin's Style II' (following the classification by the Swedish scholar Bernhard Salin). Style II, in which long-bodied beasts interlace sinuously with others or turn back upon themselves to bite their own bodies with long jaws, replaced the earlier Style I (in which the animal bodies are divided into segments, and sometimes appearing just as a jumble of limbs) early in the third quarter of the 6th century AD and continued to be used and developed until the middle of the 7th century. The presence of

Copper-alloy apex disc from a mid 6th-century AD shield boss in grave 600 at Mucking, Essex, with outline drawing of the relief-cast Style I animal ornament on the gilded central roundel | Disc scale c 2:1

Style II ornament is evidence that the assemblage was probably buried no earlier than the last quarter of the 6th century. This tallies with the evidence of the coins.

Our closest estimation of the burial date must come from the most recently manufactured items it contains. Apart from the coffin and the structure of the chamber itself, these are the gold belt buckle and gold-foil crosses, which were made specifically for the funeral and thus manufactured between death and burial. The crosses are unique items and in themselves can offer no secure date. The buckle, however, is a rare gold example of a copper-alloy type that in England and on the Continent is found in burials of the period c AD 570–620. It cannot have been buried before the coins were minted and so we can be confident that the burial dates to the period c AD 580–620. Assuming that the buckle was made a few years after the earliest possible date for the minting of the coins, that the drinking vessels had seen

Detail of the Style II ornament on rectangular panels from the Prittlewell drinking horns

Scale 1:1

at least a few years' use before they were buried, and that the buckle was made when the type was still in fashion and not declining in popularity, we can suggest that the burial dates to the period c AD 590–610. It must be stressed, however, that because of the inherent difficulties of dating purely by artefact type this narrower date range is conjecture.

THE HISTORICAL BACKGROUND AND ARCHAEOLOGICAL DATING

If the coins and grave goods leave us with a range of 20–40 years, can the historical sources help to date the burial more closely?

Our evidence is that regional kingdoms such as Kent and those of the East Angles and East Saxons were established by powerful ruling families towards the end of the 6th century AD (Chapter 1). Bede records in his *History of the English Church and people* that the East Saxons were ruled in AD 604 by a king called Saebert whose mother was Ricula, the sister of King Æthelbert of Kent. Saebert was the first Christian king of the East Saxons, converting under the influence of his Kentish uncle. Further information about Saebert's family comes from later royal genealogies. These identify six East Saxon kings or sons of kings who died between c AD 590 and 625. Saebert's father Sledd evidently died before AD 604; Saebert died c AD 616 but sources also suggest a brother, Seaxa, who probably predeceased him. Saebert's sons Saeward, Seaxred and ?Seaxbald, who ruled after him, were all killed in a battle with the *Gewisse* (later known as the West Saxons) c AD 623.

The Prittlewell gold-foil crosses are explicitly Christian symbols. Because of this it was initially assumed that the burial could not be earlier than AD 597 (when the mission of St Augustine arrived in Kent) and very probably AD 604 (the date by which Saebert had converted to Christianity). Similarly, it was thought unlikely to be later than c AD 616, when Saebert died, because after this Bede records a pagan reaction against the Christian Church among the East Saxons. It was not until the 650s, during the reign of Sigebert 'Sanctus', who had been baptised at the court of King Oswiu of Northumbria, that Christianity was firmly re-established among the East Saxons, and it was very unlikely that this collection of artefacts could have been

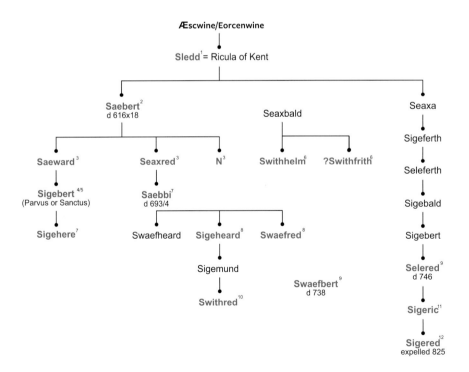

Genealogy of the East Saxon kings reconstructed from Bede's *History* and later charters and royal genealogies; kings (in red) are numbered in the order in which they ruled, including joint reigns; the place in the genealogy of one of the two mid 7th-century AD King Sigeberts (Parvus or Sanctus[4/5]) is unknown

buried as late as the middle of the 7th century. Cedd of Lastingham, who was sent to the East Saxon kingdom from Northumbria around AD 654, founded churches at Bradwell-on-Sea (*Ythancaestir*) and at Tilbury (probably East Tilbury) that may have been intended as missionary centres for the districts north and south of the River Crouch.

Bede's account, however, is specifically focused on the history of the Church. The gradual process by which knowledge of Christianity was spread, including the acquisition of artefacts with Christian associations or symbols, and the presence of individuals who had been baptised or who had lived in predominantly Christian societies on the Merovingian Continent or in north and west Britain, is a different matter from ecclesiastical history and could have taken place over a much longer period of time, beginning well before AD 597. Bede acknowledges that an important preliminary to the successful reception of Augustine's mission was King Æthelbert of Kent's marriage to the Christian Frankish princess, Bertha, which took place *c* AD 580. One of the conditions of the marriage was that Bertha was to be allowed to practise her own religion. She came accompanied by a Frankish bishop called Liudhard, who restored a church dedicated to St Martin in Canterbury for their use in the AD 580s. Thus, through his mother, Saebert – and his father Sledd – had contacts with Christianity in the circle of the Kentish court before AD 597. It is quite possible that Ricula herself had been baptised. Bede does not usually record the names of pagans, and so the fact that he names her but not Saebert's father is suggestive. There are indications, too, that the pagan reaction recorded by Bede after Saebert's death may have had as much to do with competing factions within the East Saxon ruling elite as any genuine hostility to Christianity.

There is, then, no compelling reason to link the Prittlewell grave directly to any of the dates for Bede's account of the conversion of the English and the East Saxons. A Christian burial, or one with Christian symbols, before AD 597 is not impossible, especially as the East Saxon rulers may have had close personal links with Christian circles at the Kentish court before the arrival of Augustine's mission. Similarly, there is no need to rule out a profession of Christianity in the years immediately after Saebert's death. Ultimately, the dating of the grave must depend on independent analysis of the archaeological and coin evidence.

Scientific dating

Fortunately, there are statistical and scientific techniques that allow us to model the date of the burial more accurately and rigorously.

At the same time as post-excavation analysis of the Prittlewell burial, an ambitious project was under way at Cardiff University, Queen's University Belfast and English Heritage (now Historic England) to improve the dating of early Anglo-Saxon graves and grave goods. This study of over 600 furnished inhumations (now published as *Anglo-Saxon graves and grave goods of the 6th and 7th centuries: a chronological framework*: see 'Further reading') used seriation by correspondence analysis – a computer-aided statistical method that arranges grave assemblages in order of similarity – to model how the combinations of artefact types buried as grave goods changed over time. Statistical modelling (Bayesian statistics) was then used to combine this information with the results of high-precision radiocarbon dates on human bone from key graves within the sequence. The result was a new chronological framework, consisting of sequences of phases for which there are robust calendrical date ranges whose limits are expressed to a specific degree of probability. This means that grave assemblages and individual artefact types can be assigned to defined phases with known date ranges.

Early information about the Prittlewell burial assemblage was included in the study, and according to this framework it belongs to phase AS-MD, which is dated *cal AD 565–595 to cal AD 580–610 at 95% probability* and *cal AD 570–585 to cal AD 585–605 at 68% probability*. (The date ranges are written in *italics* because this is the international scientific convention for dates that have been statistically modelled in this way.) This means that, according to the information in the model, there is a 95% probability that the Prittlewell burial was made no earlier than AD 565–95 and no later than AD 580–610, and a 68% probability that it was made no earlier than AD 570–85 and no later than AD 585–605.

During excavation there did not seem to be any possibility of obtaining scientific dates from the Prittlewell grave itself. The skeleton had not survived and so could not be radiocarbon dated, and none of the fragmentary wood remains, whether from the chamber, coffin or wooden artefacts, offered any potential for dendrochronology (tree-ring dating). During conservation and analysis, however, it became apparent that enough survived of some organic items to make radiocarbon dating by accelerator mass spectrometry (AMS), which can provide dates from very small samples, a realistic proposition.

Eight samples were submitted for AMS dating, but because of the state of preservation and the technical issues only four produced reliable dates, two from one of the drinking horns and two from one of the wooden cups. These give date ranges for the death of the animal whose horns were used, and when the wood for the cup was cut, and the burial cannot be earlier than these events.

These dates were then combined with the seriation to refine the chronological model in the light of more complete information. This result gives the date range of the chamber grave as *cal AD 575–605* (95% probability) or *cal AD 580–600* (68% probability) and the coins independently rule out a date before *c* AD 580. It is possible from this to calculate that there is a 38% probability that the burial dates to the 580s, a 45% probability that it dates to the 590s, and a 10% probability that it belongs to the 600s. The burial thus cannot be as late as the death of Saebert *c* AD 616 (a less than 1% probability). It could belong to the time of, or immediately after, St Augustine's arrival in Kent in AD 597, which would allow Christian elements in the burial practice to be explained in the context of the Augustinian mission. Against this, however, it is 80% probable that whoever is buried here died before St Augustine's arrival and, as noted above and discussed in more detail below, there are other possible explanations.

The princely burials at Taplow, Broomfield and Sutton Hoo mound 1 were also included in the national dating project. Whereas Prittlewell belongs to phase AS-MD, they are assigned to the succeeding phase AS-ME (*cal AD 580–610 to cal AD 610–645 at 95% probability*), making Prittlewell the earliest Anglo-Saxon princely burial for which we have enough information to make a confident chronological judgement. Taken with the fact that the Prittlewell burial includes the earliest archaeological evidence for Christian belief known from Anglo-Saxon England, it suggests that their ties with Kent put the ruling elites of the East Saxons at the forefront of cultural and intellectual trends in England in the last two decades of the 6th century AD.

8

What sort of person was buried?

Social identity – age, gender, status and rank

The tiny fragments of tooth enamel, which were the only remains of the skeleton to survive, could be from either a male or a female. They suggest that the person buried here was an adult or older juvenile. This is supported by the height of the deceased as inferred from the relative positions of the gold-foil crosses, belt buckle and garter buckles, which indicate someone who was either fully grown or nearing full growth, and is consistent with the size of the coffin. Any further information on the age of the deceased, and whether they were male or female, must come from the evidence of clothing, possessions and equipment found within the coffin and chamber.

Burial with weapons symbolised a masculine warrior identity in early Anglo-Saxon England, and the presence of a set of weapons – sword, shield, spears and arrow – is a sure sign that the person buried here was male. The knife in the box collection is also of a size known only from adult male burials in early Anglo-Saxon England. The weapons may also offer a clue to the age at which he died. The combination of sword, shield and spears is normally found only with adult men, over the age of 18–20 years at death, but in some cases younger males of high status were accorded this distinction, and the inclusion of a single arrow would normally mark an older child or adolescent.

Male and female clothing was distinctive and different, and served then – as now – to signal and define gender identity. Gold braid and buckled garters occur in male and female graves, but triangular-plated belt buckles are found overwhelmingly in adult male burials. Equally telling is the absence of any items such as the characteristic garnet-inlaid brooches, pendants and beads that would be expected in a high-status female burial of the late 6th or early 7th century AD. The clothing of the Prittlewell body thus also suggests a male rather than a female.

Probably the most intimate items in the chamber are the contents of the painted box – the knife and firesteel (items normally worn suspended from a belt as part of everyday dress), the spoon for eating, the comb for grooming and possibly even an undergarment. The inclusion of the cylindrical container suggests that it had a special significance for the dead person. If a reliquary, it would speak of Christian belief; if amuletic, a good-luck charm or a protection against injury or illness.

Other items from the chamber that are usually associated with male burials are the gaming equipment, lyre, east Mediterranean basin, large cauldron, drinking horns and metal-decorated wooden drinking vessels. The glass vessels, small cauldron, hanging bowl, flagon, buckets and tub are found in both male and female burials, but the provision of large numbers of vessels associated with the preparation, serving and consumption of food and drink is rare. The only other English sites where it is seen on the same scale as at Prittlewell are Taplow and Sutton Hoo mound 1, both male assemblages (although, as at Prittlewell, there is no biological confirmation of the sex of the deceased). Such provision is thus characteristic of high-status male burial in England at this time and emphasises the obligations of lordship to maintain retainers and household, and to offer generous hospitality.

The portable wealth embodied in the number and range of grave goods, and the large number of high-status items unequivocally place Prittlewell with the small group of outstandingly rich princely burials of late 6th- and early 7th-century AD England. The wealth of the burial assemblage is complemented by the resources that went into constructing the chamber and the mound. Just as the wealth of artefacts is massively greater than in contemporary weapon burials such as those in the Prittlewell cemetery – which are themselves the graves of higher-status individuals – so the construction of the chamber and mound represents an investment in labour and materials 140–150 times greater than preparation of a normal flat grave. Chamber, mound and the extreme provision of grave goods are the key elements of elite funerary practice, which was one of the ways in which new ruling groups distinguished themselves from their followers. The Prittlewell burial

Reconstruction of the burial chamber with the coffin closed and covered with cloaks, and the lamp burning at the foot end (looking west) | Artist Faith Vardy

was as much a statement about the status of his kindred as about that of the deceased individual, and about their command of portable wealth, human labour and natural resources.

Prittlewell was the burial of someone at the top of the social scale, but was he a ruler or a king? This is not an easy question to answer, partly because it is difficult to put aside the 1400 years of history that separate us from that time and have shaped our modern ideas of royalty, but comparing Prittlewell with other princely burials gives some strong indications. The Sutton Hoo ship burial, which is by a very considerable margin the richest burial known from Anglo-Saxon England, contained elaborate and costly gold-and-garnet accoutrements and regalian items such as the whetstone/ sceptre thought to symbolise kingly authority, which are not in the Prittlewell assemblage. Sutton Hoo also had a large collection of weapons and war gear – elaborately decorated helmet and shield, a mail shirt, a sword with gold-and-garnet fittings, and at least nine spears. Taplow has an elaborate gold buckle and clasps, and three shields and six spears as well as a sword. At both Sutton Hoo and Taplow the weapon assemblages have been interpreted as representing the deceased's role as head of an armed retinue and war leader, over and above the individual warrior identity symbolised by the simpler weapon sets seen at Prittlewell and in most other male burials of the time. The mound at Prittlewell was also rather smaller, and less impressive as a monument, than those at Taplow and Sutton Hoo. Mound 1 at Sutton Hoo is believed to be the burial of a king of the East Angles, possibly Raedwald (died c AD 625) who according to Bede followed King Æthelbert of Kent in having some type of lordship over other southern English kings. Taplow is thought to be the burial of a local prince or sub-king, subservient to the kings of Kent. If Sutton Hoo symbolises the roles and status of a regional king who also exercised some wider lordship, and Taplow a subordinate local ruler, then by comparison the person buried at Prittlewell, although belonging to the same social class, appears unlikely to have been a king or regional ruler.

There are, however, two items from the burial chamber that may symbolise other aspects of lordship. The folding stool can be seen as not simply an item of aristocratic furniture but as a symbol of authority. The word stool (Old English *stol*) is clearly associated with rulers in Anglo-Saxon literature. In *Beowulf* it occurs as *bregostol* (princely seat), *gifstol* (gift seat, implying its use for the seated lord to reward his loyal followers and warriors with gifts) and *ethelstol* (ancestral throne). The iron candelabrum might also be linked with a class of objects that had overtones of authority as well as status in the late Antique world. Together, then, they might symbolise in burial legal and jurisdictional aspects of lordship, rather than the military leadership that underpinned kingly power at this time.

CULTURAL IDENTITY OF THE FINDS

The Prittlewell burial was a statement by members of a new elite as to how they saw themselves and the self-images they wished to project. The objects selected for inclusion give an insight into their material world, into the range of contacts they enjoyed, and into the cultural affiliations that they chose to emphasise.

The first thing to stress is that most of the items in the burial were probably made by Anglo-Saxon craftsmen working for the person buried at Prittlewell or members of his kin, or for other aristocratic patrons who subsequently passed on items as gifts. The gold buckle was almost certainly made at Prittlewell specifically for the burial, and there is no reason to think that the weapons, wooden drinking vessels and drinking horns, the gaming set, or many of the textiles, were not made locally or in the immediate region. The iron stand and the folding stool may have been imported pieces, but both were within the technical capacity of craftsmen working in south-east England, and some features of the way the stool was constructed suggest local manufacture.

The hanging bowl was made in north or west Britain, probably originally for a Christian patron among the elite of British society, and the glass vessels are almost certainly from Kent. The latticed blue glass beakers were manufactured for the elite. They occur with certainty as pairs only in the Broomfield and Prittlewell princely burials, suggesting that they had particular significance as status markers within the top ranks of East Saxon society, and it is possible that the vessels in both burials were possessions of the same family or kin group. Single examples are recorded from the old and/or disturbed finds of Cuddesdon and Sutton Hoo mound 2. Both the hanging bowl and blue glass vessels are likely to have been acquired as gifts through the

Other items in the burial chamber may also have been intended to convey a Christian message. Of these, the flagon has the most overt Christian symbolism and was made for an eastern Mediterranean pilgrim market. It may, therefore, have had a strong symbolic value in an early Christian context in England but could, on the other hand, have been valued simply as an unusual example of the eastern Mediterranean vessels that collectively formed part of the material expression of elite identity. The same is true of the hanging bowl. It was the product of a Christian Celtic society but it was used and buried in a very different cultural context, where its symbolic significance might equally be as a prestige item and embodiment of long-distance elite contacts. The cylindrical container, if seen as a reliquary, would have Christian connotations, but not if seen as an amulet container.

Burial in a coffin with iron fittings might suggest a cultural affiliation with Kent and Christian Francia. It might be argued, too, that the two Frankish *tremisses*, with crosses on the reverse, were placed in the burial because of this Christian symbolism as well as their value as portable wealth and as markers of links with Francia. Against this, however, is the fact that nearly all Frankish coins of this period carry a cross on the reverse.

Perhaps more significant is the fact that weapons and personal items that would normally be on or near the body, whether or not in a coffin, were placed away from it. In particular, swords appear to have been so strongly linked to the personal identity of the men who were buried with them that it is almost unheard-of for the weapon not to be placed alongside or on the body, and in some cases an arm was wrapped around the sheathed weapon, hugging it to the body. The difference at Prittlewell is so marked that it suggests an intentional separation between the coffined body of someone who had died as a Christian, with the promise of resurrection, and the traditional material symbols of worldly personal identity and social roles that were represented by the burial assemblage outside and around the coffin.

This brings into focus the ways in which symbols of Christian belief at Prittlewell were conveyed through material symbols as part of the traditional burial practice of furnished inhumation. There is nothing inherently pagan about furnished burial, and Christian Anglo-Saxons continued to bury their dead with grave goods for at least a further 70 years. We see here, at the very beginning of English Christianity, how the

Detail of the cross motif on
the hanging bowl | Scale c 1:1

Detail of a miniature from the
late 6th-century AD Gospels
of St Augustine, showing
Simon of Cyrene helping
Christ carry his cross; the
part of the cross extending
behind Simon's shoulder, and
resembling the form and
proportions of the Prittlewell
crosses, is circled

Gold ring of the late 6th or
early 7th century AD from
Uttlesford in north-west
Essex, now in Saffron Walden
Museum; the arms of the
cross held by the standing
figure have flared terminals
like the gold-foil crosses from
the Prittlewell burial | Height
c 27mm

new religion was accommodated within the framework of pre-Christian and non-Christian belief that made up the broader world view of early English society. This is entirely in keeping with the advice of Pope Gregory the Great to Abbot Mellitus (who became the first Bishop of the East Saxons) in the early years of St Augustine's mission, who counselled that the Church, rather than confronting or banning traditional (pagan) festivals and symbols, should assimilate them by giving them a Christian significance. A Christian aristocrat was still an aristocrat, just as a Christian king was still a ruler and warlord, and – as is shown by the use of gold-and-garnet and Style II decoration on explicitly Christian items in the Staffordshire hoard – traditional symbols of elite wealth and status were as potent in the Christian kingdoms of the mid 7th century AD as in the pre-Christian societies of the later 6th century.

WHO WAS HE?

The person buried in the chamber grave at Prittlewell was a man, possibly a very young man, of aristocratic or princely lineage. He was a Christian convert, or buried as one, who died late in the 6th or at the very beginning of the 7th century AD. He was possibly, but by no means certainly, of the kindred of Sledd and Saebert. He or his kin almost certainly owned estates centred on what is now Prittlewell, were local if not regional power players, and enjoyed far-reaching social and political contacts. He lived at the top level of a hierarchical society, with a lifestyle supported by a sophisticated farming regime and a productive agricultural population, skilled craftspeople, and a household and retinue, and with access to imported luxuries and prestige items. He was buried with items symbolising his membership of a warrior class and his lordly authority, and the reciprocal obligations of patronage, hospitality and largesse were so important to those who buried him that they are heavily represented in the symbolism of the grave.

We do not know whether or not he ever fought in battle, delivered judgement, or presided at a feast. If he was a mature man then he had probably actively fulfilled the social roles symbolised in the burial assemblage. If he died as a young man or a juvenile then this is less likely, and in that case the symbolism of the burial assemblage would take on a compensatory aspect, representing the roles that would define someone of his lineage and status.

When discovery of the burial was first announced in 2004 there was speculation that this was the burial of an East Saxon king, with Saebert the favoured candidate. We now know that the burial is almost certainly too early to be that of Saebert, and so the only other recorded ruler with whom it might be identified is his father, Sledd. We have no reason, though, to think that Sledd was Christian, and although the burial assemblage very clearly symbolises the obligations of lordship and implies aspects of authority, it is unlikely for the reasons already discussed to be that of a king or regional ruler. Nor in fact is there any reason to think that this must be the burial of a member of the immediate family of Sledd and Saebert, rather than a member of one of the other elite kindreds who held local power among the East Saxons. These families formed the royal power base of warriors and retainers, but their names have not come down to us. The historical sources are very scanty, and not only do we hear nothing about those around the East Saxon rulers but we can also be certain that there were other members of the immediate royal family (Saebert's wife, for example) who are not recorded.

If we do feel it necessary to seek a candidate from the known family of Sledd and Saebert then the best candidate would be Saebert's brother Seaxa, who probably died before him, perhaps before he began to rule. If we follow this line of thinking, then we might consider that the person responsible for the burial and its precocious Christian elements was Ricula, Sledd's wife and Seaxa and Saebert's mother. We know very little about her, not even when she died, but she had probably been baptised and as King Æthelbert's sister she had connections with Christian circles at the Kentish court even before the arrival of St Augustine.

This is, however, highly speculative, veering into the territory of historical fiction. We do not know the name or family of the Prittlewell prince, and we almost certainly never will. We do, however, know enough to make some sense of him in his time and place, and we should not try to force the evidence by striving unnecessarily to identify him with one of the handful of individuals named in the few surviving written sources.

9

What can we say about the East Saxon kingdom?

The Prittlewell burial offers important insights into how Anglo-Saxon society was developing at the time kingdoms were being established and the Roman Church was beginning the mission to the English. With its evidence for local circumstances and for regional and international contacts, it is significant for our understanding of early Essex, early England and northern Europe. We need to set it against what we know, and what it tells us about the East Saxon kingdom and its wider connections.

Historical evidence

The East Saxon kingdom existed as a separate political entity from the end of the 6th century until the early years of the 9th century AD when it came under the control of the kings of Wessex. This relatively long history suggests that royal control was firmly founded and supported by a robust social and economic infrastructure. There is evidence, though, both for episodes of joint kingship and for internecine conflict, and there were times when the East Saxon rulers came under the influence, if not the formal authority, of other rulers, such as the powerful Wulfhere of Mercia (reigned AD 658–75). The core area of the kingdom was broadly that of the historic county of Essex but such written records as we have for the 7th century mainly refer to royal activity in the southern and eastern parts of the later county.

In the late 7th and 8th centuries AD East Saxon kings seem often to have exercised control of districts (Latin *regiones* or *pagi*) in surrounding areas, especially in what was to become Hertfordshire, Middlesex and Surrey. In the late 7th century, when East Saxon kings were at the height of their powers, overlordship extended to at least part of Kent. Although none of the East Saxon kings held power over wider areas of

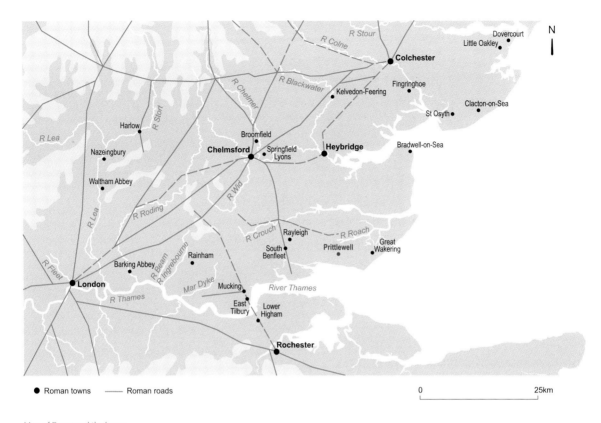

N

● Roman towns   ——— Roman roads

0   25km

Map of Essex and the lower
Thames region showing relief,
rivers, main Roman roads and
selected Anglo-Saxon sites

southern England, they were clearly a significant power in the south-east. They can be compared with the kings of Kent and the East Angles rather than with, say, the rulers of the South Saxons, whose authority seems to have been more limited and local.

Although Saebert was one of the first Anglo-Saxon kings to be baptised, his successors were not all Christians and Bede records a brief reversion to traditional non-Christian beliefs as late as the AD 660s. However, from the second half of the 7th century AD the royal house supported Christianity in the same ways as their counterparts in other Anglo-Saxon kingdoms, notably through the foundation of religious houses. The major royally-sponsored East Saxon nunneries were Barking in the south-west and Nazeingbury in the west, and there is a tradition that a third royal

nunnery was founded in the 7th century at St Osyth (formerly
Chich), south of Colchester, in the north-east of the kingdom.
There is also a tradition that the monastery at Wakering, east of
Prittlewell, was founded in the 7th century as the resting place for
the murdered bodies of two young Kentish princes. Excavation at
Great Wakering has identified evidence for 7th- to 9th-century
occupation, including two fragments from a late 8th- or 9th-
century limestone tomb shrine that may have been a replacement
for an original 7th-century wooden shrine housing the bodies of the
murdered Kentish princes. Exactly why Kentish royalty should have
been buried in the East Saxon kingdom is unclear, but at the very least
this tradition would appear to confirm continuing strong links between the royal
families of Kent and the East Saxons.

Fragment from a late 8th- or
9th-century AD limestone
tomb shrine from Great
Wakering, Essex, featuring a
serpent with interlaced body
Scale c 1:3

Geography and settlement in the region

Essex forms the north-eastern section of the lower Thames basin, which lies
between the Chilterns to the north-west and the South Downs to the south-west. To
the east the outer estuary of the River Thames forms a broad sea gulf that opens
onto the southern North Sea. The estuary is fringed by marshes, mudflats and low-
lying open beaches, by creeks and smaller estuaries, including on the north side the
Colne, the Blackwater and the Crouch. The mid Essex ridge of wooded hills, just
south of the line of the London to Colchester Roman road, separates the Boulder
Clay plateau to the north and north-west from the London Clay lowlands and the
Thames gravel terraces to the south and south-east.

Early Anglo-Saxon sites in the lower Thames region north of the river are mostly
situated along the valleys feeding into the Thames and on the intervening gravel
terraces, with relatively few sites on the higher land to the north. This was a coastal-
facing settlement region stretching from London to Colchester, linked to and bound
together by sea- and river-going routes of communication that ultimately connected
with Kent and the Continent. Within this, the known sites represent farming
communities settled along the river valleys, exploiting the range of terrains and
resources offered by the landscape and seascape.

The archaeological evidence suggests a relatively flat social structure in the 5th and earlier 6th centuries AD, but by the middle and later 6th century there is evidence from burials and chance finds for increased social differentiation and for the increasing degrees of lordship and surplus extraction (such as tribute and renders of farming produce) that this would imply. It is likely that local group identities were rooted in the physical proximity of valley settlements, and the social links that this would engender, and in their shared use of valuable local resources such as woodland and coastal marshes. It was from leadership of such local groups that wider lordship probably developed. Place-name evidence may record just such groupings. To the west, the name of the *Berecingas*, 'the dwellers among the birch-trees', is preserved in the place name Barking; the *Haeferingas*, 'the people of Haefer', in Havering; the *Yppingas*, 'the upland dwellers', in Epping and Uppingham; and the *Hrothingas*, 'the people of Hrotha', in the Rodings. In the east, the similarly-formed *Daenningas*, 'dwellers in the woodland', relates to the '*regio Deningei*' of an early 8th-century charter and was later applied to the Dengie hundred and peninsula. Two other possible examples of such names in the east are *Vange* meaning 'fen or marsh district', possibly to be located in the Thurrock peninsula, and *Gegingas* or *Ginges*, meaning 'dwellers in the district' and referring to an extensive area in the Wid valley south-west of Chelmsford.

There is as yet no direct evidence for the elite residences that must have housed the men buried at Broomfield and Prittlewell, nor for the estate centres through which their landed wealth was administered and collected. The establishment of religious houses in the 7th century AD, however, implies the existence of estates from whose

Sword and sword belt fittings from the princely burial at Broomfield, Essex: gold-and-garnet sword pyramid; gilt silver cloisonné buckle tongue base; gold strip from a ?buckle with filigree decoration | Width sword pyramid 16mm

lands they were endowed. The Broomfield and Prittlewell burials, situated north and south of the inhospitable lowlands of the London Clay, may represent two centres of lordship. This in turn might suggest two major regions of the kingdom of the East Saxons, one to the north-east based on the Chelmer/Blackwater valley (possibly extending north-east to include the Colchester area as well), and the other to the south-east based on the Roach estuary (and possibly extending westwards along the Thames estuary). Cedd's two monastic foundations of c AD 654 might be seen as being located in relation to these regions – Bradwell-on-Sea serving the north-east, and Tilbury the south. Elites in the Chelmer-Blackwater-Colchester area would be favourably placed to exploit and control communication routes and landing places along the North Sea coast, and in the southern area the linked routes and trading places along the Thames estuary.

Iron-bound tub and iron lamp from the Broomfield princely burial | Height of lamp 292mm

LOCAL COMMUNITIES IN SOUTH-EAST ESSEX

The Southend peninsula lies between the Rayleigh Hills to the west, the River Crouch to the north and the Thames estuary to the south, with coastal marshes fringing the sea to the east. It is crossed by the River Roach flowing east-north-east across the area to join the River Crouch c 5km from its mouth. The gravel terraces of the River Thames, overlain in places by brickearth, offered free-draining and productive land.

The personal name *Cana* is an element of the modern place names Canvey ('island of Cana's people', in the south-west) and Canewdon ('hill of Cana's people', in the north-east) and so this might possibly have been the region of Cana's people. Another place name that might indicate a local social group is Wakering (*Waceringas* or *Waeceringas*), 'the settlement of the sons or people of Wacor or Waecer'.

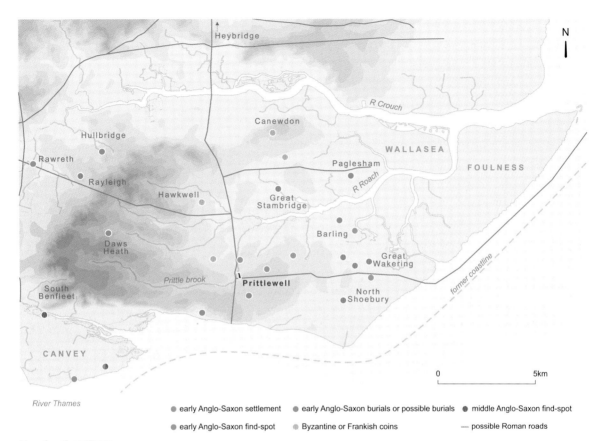

Heybridge

Canewdon

R Crouch

WALLASEA

Hullbridge

Paglesham

FOULNESS

Rawreth

Rayleigh

R Roach

Hawkwell

Great
Stambridge

Daws
Heath

Barling

Great
Wakering

Prittle brook

Prittlewell

former coastline

South
Benfleet

North
Shoebury

CANVEY

N

0   5km

River Thames

● early Anglo-Saxon settlement ● early Anglo-Saxon burials or possible burials ● middle Anglo-Saxon find-spot

● early Anglo-Saxon find-spot ⦿ Byzantine or Frankish coins — possible Roman roads

Map of south-east Essex
showing relief, possible
Roman roads and selected
Anglo-Saxon sites

The archaeology suggests a dispersed pattern of farming communities. There is
evidence for possible concentrations of settlement in the north-west around Rayleigh,
some evidence for burials in the north-east, abundant evidence for settlement
(including evidence for iron smithing and glass melting) and burials in the south-west
in the Prittle valley, burials in the south-east at North Shoebury and Wakering, and
some settlement evidence at Little Barling to the north.

The number of early Continental gold coins from the area is striking: in addition to
the two *tremisses* from the princely burial, there is another from Prittlewell parish,
one from near Southend and one from near Barling, as well as a gold *solidus* from

Hawkwell. There is also a gold sword fitting from Hullbridge. Even without the Prittlewell burial, these would suggest an elite presence and contacts with the Continent. Finds of the silver denarial coinage (sceattas) indicate that by the late 7th or early 8th century AD at least two locations on Canvey were apparently functioning as trading sites – probably as beach markets (that is, sites used temporarily as trading places during the summer months). When taken together with the Prittlewell burial and the early monastic foundation at Wakering, this might cumulatively suggest that the area was an early core of elite power that became a recognised constituent element (*regio*) of the East Saxon kingdom.

Social and economic structures

The Prittlewell burial represents the economic and social power of a leading family in a complex and sophisticated society. The economic structures of production and redistribution sustained a marked social and political hierarchy, and supported a wide range of interlinked and mutually dependent skills and specialisations. These include the agricultural, animal husbandry, extractive and land management practices that occupied the great majority of the population and generated a surplus from landed estates, the different specialisations and degrees of craft skill (from everyday blacksmithing, wood turning and weaving through food processing and production to goldsmithing, weapon crafting and production of fine textiles), and socially restricted skills, such as those of the aristocratic warrior and the bard or minstrel.

Leading families were able to accumulate and deploy this landed surplus, and to draw upon manpower, through the ties of lordship and its reciprocal obligations. In addition to their own holdings, worked by a dependent population that probably included a high proportion of slaves, such elites would have been due a proportion of any surplus from the holdings of their retainers and other free landholders, as well as taxing any external trading activity.

Like Kent and East Anglia, the early development of the East Saxon kingdom can be seen to relate in part to its favourable geographical location along the Thames estuary and the North Sea coast, giving direct access to neighbouring coastal regions and directly or indirectly to Francia, and in part to its close dynastic links to Kent in the late 6th and early 7th centuries AD. The Prittlewell assemblage illustrates just how widespread these contacts were, and how dependent the craftsmen who served elite patrons were on long-distance trade for some of their raw materials: gold from imported coinage, mercury – used in the process of gilding metal – from Spain, and garnets from as far away as India and Sri Lanka.

London, which developed to become one of the main international trading settlements of Anglo-Saxon England from the late 7th century AD, was the seat of the first Bishop of the East Saxons before he fled to safety after the death of King Saebert *c* AD 616. Control of such a critical source of power and revenue was disputed, though, and the East Saxon kings ultimately lost out to the rulers of Kent and Mercia. East of London, however, there were trading sites serving the East Saxons at Canvey and Tilbury, and there was an important centre of international commerce at Barking, probably associated with the monastic house founded by the East Saxon royal family.

There has been a tendency to underestimate the wealth, importance and sophistication of the early East Saxon kingdom. The princely burial at Broomfield has not been given the attention it deserves because the finds are incomplete and fragmentary, and because its excavation in the 1890s, which left a lot to be desired by modern standards, has still not been properly published. Some responsibility also rests with Bede, whose *History of the English Church and people* is the primary source for the 7th century AD in England. The apostate kingdom of the East Saxons in the decades following the death of Saebert was not central to his narrative of evangelisation and conversion, and subsequent historians have let his agenda influence their narratives. Discovery and analysis of the Prittlewell burial now forces us to reassess these assumptions, and to restore the East Saxon kingdom to its proper place in the world of the late 6th and 7th centuries, as an important power whose rulers were at the forefront of the social, political and cultural changes that shaped early England.

Further reading

Bayliss, A, Hines, J, Høilund Nielsen, K, McCormac, G, and Scull, C, 2013   *Anglo-Saxon graves and grave goods of the 6th and 7th centuries AD: a chronological framework* (eds J Hines and A Bayliss), Soc Medieval Archaeol Monogr 33, London

Bede   *A history of the English Church and people* (trans L Sherley-Price, rev edn 1968), Harmondsworth

Blackmore, L, Blair, I, Hirst, S, and Scull, C, 2019   *The Prittlewell princely burial: excavations at Priory Crescent, Southend-on-Sea, Essex, 2003*, MOLA Monogr 73, London

Blair, J, 2000   *The Anglo-Saxon age: a very short introduction*, Oxford

Carver, M O H (ed), 1992   *The age of Sutton Hoo: the 7th century in north-western Europe*, Woodbridge

Carver, M O H, 2017   *The Sutton Hoo story: encounters with early England*, Woodbridge

Crawford, S, with Andrews, D, 2011   *Anglo-Saxon England: 400–790*, Shire Living Histories, Oxford

Fern, C, and Speake, G, 2014   *Birds, beasts and gods: interpreting the Staffordshire hoard*, Alcester

Heaney, S, 1999   *Beowulf: a new translation*, London

Higham, N, and Ryan, J, 2013   *The Anglo-Saxon world*, New Haven and London

Leahy, K, and Bland, R, 2014 (2009)   *The Staffordshire hoard*, new edn, London

Lucy, S, 2000   *The Anglo-Saxon way of death*, Stroud

Webster, L, 2012   *Anglo-Saxon art*, London

Welch, M, 2012   A review of the archaeology of the East Saxons up to the Norman Conquest, in *The archaeology of Essex: proceedings of the Chelmsford conference* (eds N Brown, M Medlycott and O Bedwin), Trans Essex Soc Archaeol Hist 3, 110–22, Colchester

Williams, G, 2011   *Treasures from Sutton Hoo*, London

Yorke, B, 1990   *Kings and kingdoms of early Anglo-Saxon England*, London

Glass jars, wooden drinking vessels with decorative rim mounts and a drinking horn found along the east wall of the burial chamber

PLACES TO VISIT

Birmingham Museum and Art Gallery, Tamworth Castle, and The Potteries Museum and Art Gallery in Stoke-on-Trent: parts of the Staffordshire hoard on display

British Museum, London: finds from the Sutton Hoo mound 1, Taplow and Broomfield princely burials on display in Room 41

Southend Central Museum, Essex: finds from the Prittlewell Anglo-Saxon cemetery and princely burial on display

Sutton Hoo, Suffolk, the site and exhibition: The National Trust, Tranmer House, Sutton Hoo, Woodbridge, Suffolk IP12 3DJ; https://www.nationaltrust.org.uk/sutton-hoo

West Stow Country Park and Anglo-Saxon village, near Bury St Edmunds, Suffolk: www.stedmundsbury.gov.uk/sebc/play/wstow-visit-info

PICTURE CREDITS